Existential Journalism

Journalism

JOHN C. MERRILL

IOWA STATE UNIVERSITY PRESS / AMES

John C. Merrill is professor emeritus of journalism
at the University of Missouri-Columbia.

© 1996 Iowa State University Press, Ames, Iowa 50014; 1977 © John C. Merrill
All rights reserved.

∞ Printed on acid-free paper in the United States of America

First edition, 1977
Iowa State University Press revised printing, 1996

Library of Congress Cataloging-in-Publication Data

Merrill, John Calhoun
    Existential journalism / John C. Merrill.—[Rev. ed.]
      p. cm.
    Includes bibliographical references (p.) and index.
    ISBN 0-8138-2067-7
    1. Journalism—Philosophy. 2. Existentialism. I. Title.
PN4731.M43   1995
070.4'01—dc20   95-38322

This book is dedicated
to all journalism students and journalists
who respect themselves and their abilities, and who desire
to expand their personal autonomy within their media institutions,
and to all those faculty members who love freedom,
rationality, and self-determinism, and are
dedicated to instilling a sense of
purpose and action in their
students; further,
this book is dedicated to the small coterie of journalists
who break ranks with the conformists, pursue excellence, prize
independence of thought and action, and push themselves into
the invigorating complex of events and ideas
where unexpected surprises and even
dangers rise up on all sides.
In a dispirited world where
mass order and technical life are
destroying that which is human and humane,
what is needed is an existential approach by the
individual.Where leaders are scarce, life is cheap,
the family is disintegrating, and the individual is escaping
into the safe haven of organized thought and action,
journalists, as Karl Jaspers has said, must
"merge themselves in the tension and
reality of day, seeking out that
innermost region where the
soul of the age takes a
step forward"; this
takes freedom,
will, and courage. But with
these, the existential journalist
can become authentic and can change the world—
at least a small part of it. It is to this person who
loves self—and all selves—that this little book is dedicated.

CONTENTS

4 / PESSIMISM, ANXIETY, AND FREEDOM, 46

5 / INDIVIDUALISM, COMMITMENT, AND ACTION, 75

6 / IN SEARCH OF AUTHENTICITY, 96

7 / POSTSCRIPT: *CARPE DIEM*, 117

FOREWORD

On the book publishing scene of the 1990s, when many books are as perishable as fresh flowers, the revival of a volume that appeared nearly two decades ago is a rare event. That happens only when the book, in this instance John Merrill's *Existential Journalism,* is deemed to be important and enduring, which it is.

To consider *Existential Journalism,* in this fresh and revised printing, is to enter a vital and vigorous argument about the role of the journalist as an individual in an increasingly corporate and bureaucratic communications industry. John Merrill, one of journalism education's most gifted scholar-teachers, knows and understands well the connections between journalism and public life. In this book, he draws on philosophy, specifically existentialism, as an underpinning and framework for confronting the pragmatic and sometimes ugly realities faced by journalists. This book, with its puzzling and abrupt title, *Existential Journalism,* starts arguments. When it was first published in 1977, it garnered a strong response. Scholars familiar with Professor Merrill's writings immediately saw it as an extension of his elegant and measured study, *The Imperative of Freedom,* while others in the academy and industry confessed ignorance about "existential journalism" or denounced the idea as pretentious.

John Merrill—at once the serious student of the media and ever the provocateur and prankster—enjoyed the fuss his new book caused. The more strident the reaction, the more likely that the book would stimulate discussion, which is exactly what Merrill wanted to do. He might have secretly hoped his exploration into the literature of journalism and philosophy would provoke his readers to explore the original sources from philosophy and literature on which he draws. Those whose memories of college philosophy courses were hazy needed to scramble back to the library to be sure that they were in touch with Professor Merrill's ideas and vocabulary. In a sense, then, the book is a well-planned strategy (some would say ploy) to raise the role of the individual in the media organization to a high and useful level of discussion.

Existentialism, one dictionary instructs, is "a philosophy that emphasizes the uniqueness and isolation of the individual experience in a hostile or indifferent universe, regards human experience as unexplainable, and stresses freedom of choice and responsibility for the consequences of one's acts." For journalists, existential journalism is the connecting tissue between complete and unconstrained freedom and responsible action.

At the time this book first appeared, journalists in North America were engaged in a lively debate over the New Journalism, a journalistic-literary movement mainly in magazines that promoted the use of literary devices and even urged advocacy. That was a departure from the theory of objective journalism, which was tied to a clinical separation of fact and opinion where possible, or at least an effort at impartiality, especially in matters involving politics, economics and public life more generally. At the same time, this trend toward impressionistic and more subjective journalism lived alongside computer-assisted reporting and precision journalism, which encouraged the use of social science research techniques in reporting as well as the quantification of much of the news. Both of these trends were happening inside media organizations, especially newspaper companies and electronic media firms that were large, impersonal and growing still larger.

In the intervening years, journalism in print and electronic media has grown more sensational and more likely to be interpretative. The political scientist Thomas Patterson decried this predisposition to interpretation and even bias, especially in political news, as journalism "out of order" and unnecessarily subjective. News seems to be caught up in wretched excess as seen on tabloid television shows and in other sensation-seeking media.

In a study in which Merrill invokes the ideas of Søren Kierkegaard, Karl Jaspers, Martin Heidegger, Jean-Paul Sartre and Albert Camus, who charted the individual in endgame movements with the universe and life itself, he returns always to the difficult dilemma for the journalist who clings to creativity and individual choice even in a cumbersome and bureaucratic organization. He argues that journalists can have a personal imprint, a career signature on their work, their colleagues and the organization in which they work. Two decades ago, this argument was best made in the West, where freedom of expression based on concepts from the

Enlightenment was alive and well, even in corporate media environments. Individuals could still be individuals in the choices they made, whether that meant conformity or a break with the status quo. In totalitarian systems (both communist regimes and military dictatorships), individualism had a more difficult time as the stakes were higher and usually more punitive. Still, even in the most repressed societies, freedom of expression and journalistic fire existed—sometimes well underground, sometimes in defiance of the state. Today in most of the world, there is a trend toward democratization and market economies—a process which has largely ended censorship and ushered in a new era of media freedom and reportorial independence. Nonetheless, there is self-censorship, both in the large media corporations of the West and in the most visible news organs in Asia, Africa and Latin America.

The journalist of the 1990s and of the dawn of the 21st century faces a paradox, however. There is a trend toward concentration of ownership and media convergence, making media enterprises larger and larger and usually diminishing the influence of any single individual, especially journalists. And there is at the same time a complex system of microcommunication as seen on the Internet or in the realm of desktop publishing where empowerment for the journalists, the course, and the reader or viewer is greatly enhanced.

To be sure, the conditions under which existential journalism exists—where it does—suggest that individual action still plays a key role in communication enterprises, from the lively and creative minds of young reporters to the leaders of media companies, who live by their wits in a high-stakes game. By definition, journalism is a group activity, where consensus of some sort is essential for the product put forth for public consumption. Individuals today are being called upon to contribute ideas for new media forms and writing styles, not to mention graphic presentations.

Individual initiative in an entrepreneurial sense is encouraged. This activity occurs in an environment where moral and ethical decisions must be made hourly and where the speed of communication mitigates against hard thought. Still, talk of ethics is heard almost everywhere around the world where, as the stakes in communication change, new temptations abound. Journalism, once a raffish and badly paid craft, has achieved a new respectability, and the most prominent journalists are public figures who can command large fees on the speaker's circuit. The challenges of existential journalism again offer a template against which the problems of modern journalistic practice for individuals, whether they are reporters, editors, news sources or news consumers, can be thoughtfully examined.

When John Merrill was invited to prepare a new printing of this book—a task that necessitated substantial addition—he must have asked himself whether it was worth doing. Happily, he determined that the "payoff," which will be to ignite more small fires of human discourse, would ultimately have value. The book he has produced is provocative, stimulating and definitely worth the reader's journey through its pages. What appears here has value for anyone engaged in journalism (or who wishes to be) as well as journalism's growing "constituent assembly" of readers, listeners and viewers.

New York City, 1995   EVERETTE E. DENNIS
                              Executive Director
                              The Freedom Forum Media Studies Center

INTRODUCTION

An independent journalist always has to be willing to
offend his following.
                                    —I.F. STONE, 1988

I.F. Stone's death in 1989 was the symbolic end to a decade in
which existential journalism was seriously undermined by corporate conglomerates and collectivist thought. In one of the many
tributes to Stone's life, Fred Friendly, the legendary CBS executive, called Stone "the conscience of investigative journalism."
Others—from William F. Buckley on the right to Victor Navasky
on the left—praised Stone for his individualism, his writing and
his existential spirit. The decade, which incidentally followed the
first edition of *Existential Journalism* in 1977, was a period in
which Stone's self-described style of competitive "maniacal zest
and idiot zeal" surrendered to media buyouts, monopolization and
the practice of "feel good" journalism. A review of some of the
events of the 1980s should explain, in part, why this new printing
of *Existential Journalism* is so important.

First, the nation has lost more than a dozen competitive newspaper markets, with some important cities dropping into the abyss
of monopoly—Baltimore, Los Angeles, Little Rock, Shreveport,
Columbus, Philadelphia. Two other large cities, Dallas and San
Antonio, were lost to monopoly early in this decade, and in Detroit
two of the largest news conglomerates, Gannett and Knight-Ridder, entered into a government-sanctioned joint operating agreement. Second, the three television networks were purchased in
rapid succession by large corporate interests whose first moves to
cope with highly leveraged debt included massive cuts in news
budgets. For the first time, broadcast news operations were

aligned as profit centers that had to *produce* revenue to justify their existence. Finally, large corporate news interests, again such as Knight-Ridder and Gannett, formulated hiring and merit policies that demand "right-thinking" (or like-thinking) employees, moving civic harmony to the top of the media's list of functions, practices and obligations. Editors were told that new hires would have to put community above all else, while educators, following the corporate example, began producing ethics textbooks and manuals incorporating ideas of communitarian philosophy.

Izzy Stone, of course, never would have bought into all of this. As an up-and-coming New York editorial writer who had founded his first radical paper at the age of 14, Stone was blacklisted in the communist Cold War purges that eventually sent American journalism into a serious, if unfruitful, reassessment of its traditional standard of objectivity. He relinquished membership in the National Press Club in the 1940s after waiters there refused to serve his African American lunch guest, U.S. District Judge William H. Hastie. In 1952, Stone set off to start his own paper and for two decades he ran one of the capital's most influential journals, *I.F. Stone's Weekly.* He helped launch careers of new and independent journalists, many of whom, like Peter Osnos of the *Washington Post,* never forgot his recalcitrance and righteous indignation. Early on, Stone caught the Atomic Energy Commission in a series of lies about the safety of underground nuclear testing. In the mid-1960s, he exposed the invented attack on American warships that, embellished, led to the congressional blank check for Lyndon Johnson's escalation of the war in Vietnam.

During those tumultuous times, Stone often told students that they could not understand the word "revolution" unless they first studied the Federalist Papers, which were influenced by the French Revolution, which was influenced by a Greek revolution. Truth, Stone posited, was a thread that one should not untangle at a whim or for a selfish purpose. "Power to the people?" he once said in a rhetorical echo to a group of rebellious students. "Hell, if the people ever came to power, we'd all be in jail." Nat Hentoff, a friend and neighbor, wrote that Stone admonished students not to depend on the First Amendment to change society. Hentoff quotes Stone: "All you can do, if you're lucky, is change the odds a little."

In the years before his death, Stone completed a lengthy project in which he learned Greek to research *The Trial of Socrates,* a highly acclaimed critical analysis of the Athenian democracy's treatment of the great philosopher-teacher. And, after declining their advances for three decades and rejecting their attempts at apology, Stone accepted an invitation to rejoin the Press Club. Perhaps more than other examples John Merrill gives in this book, Stone exhibited all of the important components outlined by philosopher Søren Kierkegaard: freedom, commitment, action and responsibility. Kierkegaard believed that existentialism required a large measure of independence and a willingness to take chances for what is right and just. Above all, though, he thought existentialists should be true to themselves.

Enlightenment philosopher John Locke asserted that persons develop into society as a move from individualism to corporatism. But the collective "body politic" is willed by the community, which is responsible for protecting the person and the person's extensions—life, health, labor, estates and possessions. Essentially, Locke was arguing for natural rights first, corporate individual second. Liberty, even as important as Locke considered it to the individual, carried responsibility and accountability.

Today's journalists and journalism/mass communications students would do well to adopt Kierkegaard's constructs and Locke's principles. They also should study the careers of people like Stone, journalists who, despite attempts to dull their spirits, hold their position and defend it without compromising individual freedom and integrity. Espousing such philosophy in some of today's newsrooms may be dangerous, but those practitioners and students with a commitment to action, freedom and responsibility have no other choice. As Kierkegaard, Jean-Paul Sartre and Albert Camus might tell us, finding a new career option may be more comfortable than living within the rigid confines of corporate journalism.

Before indulging the reader in examples of today's existential journalists, it is important to note a significant difference between what is being advocated here and what is commonly called "literary journalism," or what some used to call "new journalism." Existential journalism is based in individual autonomy, which means that *all* are free from tyranny and the individual cannot force others to act as she or he would desire them to act. Existential journalism assumes that no individual has power over any other individual; existential journalists only have power over themselves. Literary journalism has nothing to do with philosophy; it is concerned with technique and style, a blending of narrative that includes what Jon Franklin and other practitioners/educators call "story grammar." It is possible, of course, for an *existential* journalist to be a *literary* journalist. One could argue, for example, that Gay Talese, Norman Mailer or Tom Wolfe fit both categories, but as far as definitions are concerned, these journalisms are mutually exclusive.

What is most unfortunate, however, is the fact that only one of these—literary journalism—gets any treatment in university-level curricula. In fact, the University of Oregon and the University of Pittsburgh have established separate degree programs for literary journalism; other schools are watching these experiments closely, no doubt in anticipation of offering something similar in the future. There is no such program for existential journalism; indeed, it seldom is taught as a unit in reporting or ethics courses. The desire to produce journalists to fill the jobs at conglomerate and chain-owned newspapers and media outlets leads to molding students into conformist workers, automatons who can make news into a profit center whose chief social concern is becoming the maestro in a civic symphony. Students often are told that personal autonomy must be subjugated by "accepted" journalistic practices, personal responsibility by social responsibility.

But such a communitarian philosophy of collective responsibility plays right into the hands of a corporate community that does not play by the same ethical rules as do the practicing journalists. Corporate owners use sophisticated legal and political means to buy, sell and close their properties, with no discussion of what may be best for the communities of readers or journalists. It has been nearly a half century since the last metropolitan daily newspaper was founded and survived in an American city, but plenty have been shuttered for simple corporate convenience or at the first whiff of the spoils of monopoly. What we have seen is corporate journalism lamely responding to collectivism with more collectivism. Under that philosophy, one newspaper in a metropolitan area is *always* better than two.

Long ago, Karl Jaspers wrote that the mass society and its machinelike instrumentation was robbing the soul of humans and humanity. Grounding his argument in Kierkegaard and Nietzsche, Jaspers lamented individuals escaping into collectivist thought, adopting the "we" keyword of the masses. Jaspers, although not a pessimist, did not believe that his philosophical construct could work in a society that seemed to be treating freedom as a passing fancy, somewhere between nature and the modern technology. Jaspers, who wrote eloquently about existential journalism, believed it was most important for journalists to resist the temptation of sensationalism and the tendency to follow a corporate line.

The most recent example of such thinking in journalism comes from William Greider, a former *Washington Post* reporter, who has written three of the most important books on journalism during the past 15 years. Greider, in fact, left the *Post* and joined *Rolling Stone* magazine for very existentialist reasons. In his most recent book, *Who Will Tell the People,* Greider wrote that the *Post* was practicing a condescending type of "hip social science—a fast-moving kind of pop sociology." The book, which posits that the Beltway concept of "gridlock" is a hoax, uncovers primary material that never would have made it into the *Post* because it demonstrates that politics in the capital has become as automatized and homogenous as daily journalism. Indeed, Greider writes, government is enmeshed in a Machiavellian piece of civic machinery that jams the democratic process by cosmetic and well-financed consensus. The same lobbyists represent and bankroll both parties, much the same as the Washington law firms who represent professional journalism organizations at the same time as they successfully negotiate market monopolies for news conglomerates who must petition the Justice Department's antitrust division. No one is wrong if everyone is right.

It should come as no surprise that Greider, who also produced an expose on the Federal Reserve, has joined the wave of independent journalists who are finding books and magazines to be their most fruitful publication venues. Greider, for instance, first published his findings on David Stockman, the banking crisis and Ronald Reagan's "trickle down" economics in the *Atlantic.* His *Post* colleagues, E.J. Dionne and Thomas and Mary Edsall, wrote two other powerful works in book form: *Why Americans Hate Politics* and *Chain Reaction,* respectively. Another *Post* employee, Bob Woodward, has written a half dozen investigative books since he and Carl Bernstein achieved fame in their coverage of the Watergate scandal. But it is Greider who has emerged as the existential journalist of the decade, the person who maintains the standard so carefully nurtured and passed along by Izzy Stone. Greider's solutions for social problems have much to do with grass roots organizing, the kind so admired by Alexis de Tocqueville when he toured America 150 years ago. Still, Greider asserts, that effort, which many may see as collectivist, comes from a corporate bureaucracy empowered *by* people *for* people, not the power brokers who play both sides of the issue just to cover their bets. Journalism, too, must be a gamble, and Greider, like Stone before him, has helped future journalists even the odds.

In daily newspaper journalism, there is one existential journalist who courageously continues to practice her craft—Molly Ivins. She is special, not only because she is a quintessential and committed Texan, but because she survived one of the recent monopolization efforts with unabashed and principled confidence. When her paper, the *Dallas Times Herald,* closed in December 1991, Ivins vowed she would not go to work for the competition, the *Dallas Morning News,* because she had too many memories of the nearly 15-year battle by two newspapers that, story for story, had blessed a city with better daily journalism than it probably deserved. On most days, in fact, it was hard to find better journalism being practiced anywhere in America. Ivins's feeling for her former rivals left her with two options within a state she did not want to leave. Her first choice was the *Houston Chronicle*; her second, the *Fort Worth Star-Telegram.* She told top editors at the *Chronicle* that she would come for a dollar more a year than she was making at the *Times-Herald.* Ivins was not starving on her income, but she certainly was not the most highly paid reporter or columnist in Dallas or Austin, her traditional base at the Texas statehouse. Indeed, having Ivins on board was an exciting prospect for the *Chronicle,* which considered itself an emerging force in the state against the *Morning News.* When it came time to approve the deal, however, the *Chronicle* balked, saying it feared her autonomous and liberal orientation might upset some readers and, no doubt, some advertisers and sources. Ivins now is a columnist at the *Star-Telegram.*

Ivins, Stone and Greider made critical and committed choices to serve journalism in a spirit that did justice to their individuality. Ivins and Greider share few solutions to *society's* problems, but both probably would say that the media have done their part in putting American culture and society in a bind. At the same time, neither believes it is journalism's sole responsibility to rebuild the republic. Newspaper and broadcast conglomerates devise strategies for restructuring society, making their properties responsible for the social, moral and psychological crisis gripping the country. In this incessant worship of "we," newspapers count bylines as a measure of performance and the number of minority sources on the front page as a measure of diversity.

The existential philosophy also is becoming increasingly important because of the exponential growth of computer communication and the beginnings of a culture of personal journalism not seen in almost two centuries. Each day, people without training in the craft enter into cyberdiscourse against mainstream media, proclaiming their brand of personal journalism more truthful and honest than the corporate journalism being practiced in the monopolized markets of America. Sadly, they may be right, but as Stone pointed out, power to the people is as unworkable as giving up your personal freedoms for the sake of society. Jaspers might be impressed somewhat with the existential qualities of the computer medium, the individual's capacity to "publish" with freedom from interference by social or governmental institutions. He would not, however, see the wisdom of cyberfreedom without its incumbent responsibility. The rush to the Internet is a charge to the front by masses affluent enough to own a computer and modem. But these people, like most mainstream journalists, are joiners in groups that further restrict their individuality.

Unfortunately, many journalists have become automatons, taking their direction from nose counters who have every race and ethnic group in the readership crosshairs. That and aggressive minority hiring programs fulfill the corporate responsibility to diversity and pluralism. More and more managers are demanding that prospective reporters and editors adhere to certain communitarianlike principles *before* they even apply, a blind commitment that ignores existential journalism's emphasis on diversity of thought. The pressures to conform to the desires of the faceless ownership of today's mass media make it difficult to practice existential journalism, and we are certain that only a few will take the risks associated with becoming active and autonomous. As working professionals and students alarmed by increasing emphasis on collectivism and communitarianism in the newsroom as well as the academy, we believe existential philosophy is the key to preserving pluralistic journalism. It is a philosophy of journalism built on a simple formula: freedom, commitment, action, responsibility.

Why should we practice or teach anything else?

FRED BLEVENS
Texas A&M University

KYLE COLE
Baylor University

Existential Journalism

1

The Time Is Now

THIS BOOK was first published in 1977 and caused consternation to many of my colleagues in journalism education. Their contention: It would give journalism students dangerous ideas about freedom, making them think that being mavericks was good, causing them to shun responsibility and making them dissatisfied with the conformity urged upon them by the institutionalized media. Most of my colleagues at the time knew little or nothing about existentialism, although it had swept in from Europe about mid-century and had had considerable impact on literary and academic thought generally.

After the turbulent sixties, I suppose critics of *Existential Journalism* were anxious for things to settle down, for students to think more about conforming to institutional norms, and for journalists to think more about the concept of a socially responsible press proposed so strongly by the Hutchins Commission in 1947. Actually, I had written *Existential Journalism* largely to celebrate some of the liberal concepts of the much older European Enlightenment, to extol libertarianism, personal autonomy, individualistic action, and personal acceptance of responsibility. In short, I wished to emphasize one strain of American journalism that had always been important, but had, in my opinion, begun to be subsumed by the new emphasis on journalism's duties and responsibilities. The first edition I dedicated to Tom Wicker and Daniel Schorr, two American journalists I felt personified the spirit of existential journalism. Today's students, bombarded on all sides with entertainment-oriented personalities on talk shows, syndicated columnists, engaging TV anchors, and print and electronic tabloidism, probably aren't too well acquainted with those two. They might well sandwich Sam Donaldson and Geraldo Rivera—

even Oprah Winfrey or Rush Limbaugh—into a list of freedom-loving activists who could be considered existentialists. But such entertainment-oriented, publicity-courting figures as these are a far cry from what I really mean by an "existential journalist" and I hope that by the time you have finished these pages, you will understand why. Better nominees for existential journalism's roll would be Bill Moyers, Larry King, Hodding Carter III, Molly Ivins, and Georgie Anne Geyer. But even these are not as good exemplars of existentialism as such stalwarts of the past as I.F. Stone, Marguerite Higgins, Harry Golden, A.J. Liebling, and H.L. Mencken.

Dozens of other journalists operating today—most of them out of the national spotlight—can be considered existential journalists. Some of them are mentioned by former journalists (and now academics) Fred Blevens and Kyle Cole in their introductory essay. And, of course, any of you—especially after finishing this book—can provide other names.

Freedom: Need for a Re-emphasis

In this book I tried to place journalistic "freedom" in a central place—not just *press* freedom (the media's freedom vis-à-vis government), but especially the freedom of the individual journalist vis-à-vis the "media system." Although this was a new emphasis in journalism books, it was nothing more than the projection of the "press freedom" tradition to *individual journalists.* Some reviews at the time, along with numerous comments from journalists and journalism educators, pointed out that such an existential emphasis posed a danger. In their minds lurked the suspicion—perhaps planted there during the unruly sixties with the counterculture and youth revolution—that "radical" journalists who were trying to upset traditional values (and even the society itself) were those interested in existentialism. They remembered many of the youthful—and some not so youthful—rioters and dissidents, including many "underground" newspaper writers who had referred to themselves occasionally as "free spirits" (existentialists?). So, to many readers of the 1977 edition of this book, I was encouraging anarchy in journalism (or worse) and filling the heads of students with erroneous and dangerous ideas. These critics were mainly reacting to their concepts of the term *existentialism,* not having known very much about its elucidation by European founders and popularizers.

The purpose of the book was, and is in this new edition, to give an emphasis to *ethical* and responsible journalism, but from an individualistic or existentialist philosophical perspective. It is true that it emphasizes the virtues of freedom, individualism, and humanism. But it does not suggest irresponsibility. Contrary to what many people seem to think, one can stress freedom without condoning irresponsibility.

The book, first published by Hastings House, went out of print in the early 1980s, but was still in considerable demand by journalism students. All through the eighties and even today, I receive letters from students and former students asking where they can get a copy. Of all the books I have written, *Existential Journalism* seems to have had the greatest appeal for, and impact on, students. The thrust of the book—the importance of freedom, courage, action, and the acceptance of responsibility—struck a responsive note.

Existentialism at Century's End

As the century draws toward its close, it is appropriate that this book is re-issued in a slightly revised form. It is a time when societal pressures still tend to depreciate individual autonomy and mold journalists into smooth-functioning robots. It is my belief that journalists must rebel against this growing conformism, must push back the encroaching bonds of institutionalization and professionalization, and determine to exercise maximum freedom in their daily endeavors.

Today as communitarianism clambers into the intellectual driver's seat, at least in academic communications circles, a book with the emphasis of *Existential Journalism* is needed more than ever. With the liberalism of the Enlightenment under fire from the new communitarians (e.g., Amatai Etzioni, Christopher Lasch, Alasdair MacIntyre, and Clifford Christians), there is a need to restate the old libertarian verities so popular in intellectual circles of the seventeenth and eighteenth centuries. This is not to suggest that Enlightenment liberalism is synonymous with existentialism, for it is not, but that the eighteenth-century liberals and the more recent existentialists have had a similar respect and desire for personal freedom.

The position I am taking in this book is neither easy nor popular. It goes against the new spirit of community—or at least it will be seen by many to do this. But what is needed, I think, is for a philosophical wedge to be driven into the literature of American journalism that will cause students and others to re-examine the relevance of libertarianism both to the press system as a whole and to the individual journalist.

The attempt is made here to describe an *existential journalism* and to further bring the term into the legitimate (that is, respectable) terminology of journalistic discussion. The intent is to construct the basic framework of an existential journalism, and in so doing to provide examples of the spirit of the genre by passionately exhibiting (at least in spots) what I am talking about.

EJ's Appeal to Students

Unfortunately, existentialism is largely as misunderstood—or totally ignored—in the United States today as it was in 1977. For many, it conjures up thoughts of hedonism or anarchy, or is equated with a philosophy that justifies any and all immorality. It is, of course, not such a philosophy at all; rather, it is a description of human freedom, and it explicitly requires and sets forth at every step a theory of responsibility and morality that shapes and gives life to human freedom. I have even imbued my brand of existential journalism with a firm foundation of rationalism, something not always found in discussions of the subject.

I am happy to say that many students have resonated to the message of this book, and it is good that the small volume will be in print again so that a new generation of students can at least have access to modern-day echoes of the Enlightenment spirit of freedom and the positive aspects of existentialism. And it should be emphasized that it is not a "negative" freedom that existential journalism (or "EJ," as students often refer to it) touts, but it is an action-oriented freedom that stresses living fully and acting in such a way that a person is self-constructed—that existence really means the creation of a personal essence.

When I have lectured about or discussed existential journalism with students through the years, I have been rewarded by their instantaneous interest in the perspective; they seem to be almost stunned that somebody is stressing such a philosophy of *individual* journalistic freedom, commitment, and authenticity. Their reaction often is similar to a plant, which after a long drought, suddenly flowers with the coming of rain. They literally soak in the emphasis on integrity, authenticity, and creativity, and they are often visibly moved by the focus on *personal* journalism—the involvement of one's total Self in the enterprise, with passion and dedication, where action is decisive and responsibility is personally accepted.

Two of my graduate students at Missouri, Fred Blevens and Kyle Cole, encouraged me to consider re-issuing *Existential Journalism*. The main parts of the original book are still here, the only change being that the old Chapter 1 (Voices from Newsroom and Academe) and old Chapter 7 (Back to Newsroom and Academe) are gone. Actually those chapters were peripheral to the first edition and their repeated inclusion would only serve to date the book. Everette Dennis, executive director of the Freedom Forum Media Studies Center in New York, has written a new

Foreword to replace the earlier one by George Gordon of Hofstra University. Blevens and Cole have written an Introduction to this new edition, and I have written two new parts: this first chapter and the final chapter, Postscript: *Carpe Diem.*

It should be stressed anew that, although most journalists know little about existentialism, they seem somehow to be prejudiced against it. They see it as an irresponsible orientation. Journalism professors, rather strangely, tend to have a similar antipathy in spite of their avowed dedication to freedom of the press. And what is unfortunate, in my opinion, is that existentialism is often seen as an undisciplined, even nihilistic, emphasis that keeps students from fitting harmoniously into the modern world of corporate journalism. And many of these professors proceed to prejudice their students against its basic thrust—even if they don't refer specifically to "existentialism."

Rebellion Against Conformity

I contend that, to a greater degree than in 1977, most journalists (and journalism professors) are basically status quo persons; at least they are psychological collectivists and organization persons (in spite of their "liberal" political pretensions), suspicious or afraid of the self and the stimulation and creativity that comes from individual-oriented journalism. This kind of journalism—that is, *existential* journalism—is often seen by them as a danger because it rocks the corporate boat and endangers the smooth-running cooperative journalistic "community."

It is against this idea of mass-oriented, organizational, depersonalized, conformist type of journalism that this volume takes its stand. What we need is more emphasis on the individual journalist, on personal freedom and personal responsibility. In the last several decades we have paid enough attention to the *journalistic system,* to the *mass media,* and to the media owners and managers themselves. We seem overly concerned about the media retaining freedom from government or from other outside forces, but we rarely focus on the individual journalist who has become hardly more than a robotized functionary of increasingly corporate journalism. It is on this individual journalist that the following pages concentrate.

Let me make it clear, however, that I am no more optimistic about the individual journalist becoming an existentialist than I was when the first edition came out in 1977. Most journalists will continue to sail placidly on in their comfortable, safe, lifeless, nonexistential worlds, conforming and doing the same old things in virtually the same old ways—with ever-improving technology to distract them. Only a few hearty souls will experience the exhilarating spirit of existential journalism, and this number will be so small that the media managers and businesspeople who increasingly run journalism will not need to worry about a breakdown of their "systems."

Nonexistential journalism will continue to be the rule in the United States (and the entire world); conformity will continue to grow, along with the media groups, chains, and conglomerates; and armies of young people will swarm out of journalism (or mass communications) programs, eagerly seeking employment, gladly sacrificing individual authenticity to adapt nicely to the highly regimented, depersonalized corporate structure. Sitting comfortably before their rows of computer screens, steeped ever more deeply in technological regimentation, they will spread their creative impotence to an ever more stupefied audience. They will, in essence, have died and been buried in the giant graveyards of modern establishment journalism. They will have their reward and their peace.

And they will join their older brothers and sisters of corporate journalism in pouring out for mass consumption large amounts of garbage: sensational and unsynthesized bits and snippets of this-and-that—much of it brainless, illiterate, superficial, and meaningless—created chiefly for the entertainment-hungry, the lazy, and the thoughtless. There is something wrong with today's journalism that is produced by this mechanistic corps of nonexistentialists; we all know it, but we have trouble articulating just what is wrong—or we refuse to admit openly how shallow and vapid American journalism really is.

Lonely Rebel with a Conscience

The existential journalist rebels against being buried in this shallow mass grave. This individualistic and freedom-loving journalist has an attitude of commitment, of rebellion, of individuality, of creativity, and of freedom. The existential journalist is committed to personal standards, not to the often asinine rules and practices of the organization. He or she pushes, straining constantly against the encompassing institutional restrictions that have their dehumanizing effect. Although this journalist has a conscience or a moral sense, this does not translate into worshipping strict professionalism or institutionalism; more important for the existential journalist is a sense of self-esteem and self-reliance. This journalist revels in the ethical code that is personally internalized, not in the framed corporate code hanging on the wall. The existentialist stands, chooses, acts, and is willing to take the consequences of these choices and actions. This is often painful.

The existential journalist is alone, at times penalized by stagnation of position, pay, and newsroom status and may even be dismissed. But this journalist truly lives, creating all the while an authentic Self. No simple *thing* fitting snugly into the system, this existential journalist pushes on toward self-enhancement, believing that good individual journalists make for a good journalism. The existential journalist's lot is a difficult one today, to be sure. Only occasionally will he or she be appreciated and rewarded by those in authority. But, of course, the existential journalist *always* gets a reward—the reward of existence, of truly living. Willing, choosing, acting, committing, accepting responsibility—it is thus that he or she progresses, becoming a real person.

Journalism of Engagement

Journalistic "engagement" is the main thing. It has to do with involvement; it is the opposite of "standing apart from"; Jean-Paul Sartre certainly stresses this: the existentialist is not a *disinterested* person, but is one who is involved, participating, feeling. But this surely does not mean that he or she is satisfied to cooperate thoughtlessly for the sake of participating. For Sartre and other existentialists, the key point is that truly being human is to be engaged; one must rebel at the idea of "standing at a distance." Existential journalism is not isolating oneself, trying to be some kind of recluse or seeking shelter in a collective will; rather, it is plunging into dangerous waters and being willing to take chances.

Imitation is not engagement. It is a cop-out; it is the way the feeble and the unimaginative do their journalism. Certainly it is a comfortable and easy way; that is one reason it is so widely embraced. Listen to Eric Hoffer, the longshoreman-philosopher, writing about imitation in *The True Believer*:

> Imitation is often a shortcut to a solution. We copy when we lack the inclination, the ability or the time to work out an independent solution. People in a hurry will imitate more readily than people at leisure. Hustling thus tends to produce uniformity.

Imitation is certainly related to conformity; those who imitate easily also tend to conform easily. Again, Hoffer writes that "people whose lives are barren and insecure seem to show a greater willingness to obey than people who are self-sufficient and self-confident." This tendency to obey, to imitate, and to conform is very strong in society; and it is not strange that it is strong among journalists. Aldous Huxley said (in *Brave New World Revisited*) that there is a basic Will to Order among people, and this is actually dangerous. It "can make tyrants out of those who merely aspire to clear up a mess," and he also observed that "the beauty of tidiness is used as a justification for despotism." Huxley goes on to say that too much organization transforms men and women "into automata, suffocates the creative spirit and abolishes the very possibility of freedom."

The existential journalist rebels against this Will to Order and against what William Whyte (in *The Organization Man*) has called the "New Social Ethic." Whyte says the key words in this ethic are *adjustment, adaptation, socially oriented behavior, team work, group loyalty, group dynamics, group thinking,* and *group creativity.* I could add two others especially pertinent to the field of journalism: *media loyalty* and *professional spirit.*

Passionate vs. Dispirited Journalism

Perhaps the journalist, as much as anyone in our society, is in a position to lose selfhood and conform to what Lewis Yablonski in his book *Robopaths* has called "robopathy." The journalist may feel creative, but the nature of corporate journalism routinizes him or her into patterns of activity devoid of creativity, challenge, spontaneity, and potency. Such a journalist works, mechanically (or mechanistically) day after day without showing many—if any—sparks of creativity and passion. In fact, lack of passion—a *dispassionate* demeanor—is what defines this journalist's natural state.

Journalists of the type just described have either been educated to be dispassionate and routinized, or they have learned very quickly on the job in the newsroom. They learn "the way things are done"; they do them that way, and the work flow moves smoothly along. They are not pained or troubled by unorthodox activities which create tensions and frictions. These they have learned well to evade. Life, they believe, is simpler, more enjoyable, more placid, and less hectic if they conform. In addition, they will not be pained by making mistakes and errors in judgment. And, what is more, they will more than likely be rewarded for being a good and cooperative team player.

Such persons as these are the typical nonexistential journalists. Their number is legion. They conform. They make the usual marks; they interview with the "normal" questions; they write the regular 5-W leads and work their story into the standard inverted pyramid form or some other newer feature-hook gimmick. They submit their work to editors who "correct" it—modifying it in many ways, from subtle distortion to denuding it of its basic and original significance and meaning (if it had any).

The nonexistential journalists accept this state of affairs without protest—and continue to produce their rigid, superficial pieces with machinelike efficiency. They are, in effect, living inauthentic lives as journalists; not only they, but the editors who correct their copy, are locked into a system that denies their humanity and authenticity and enthrones routine and efficiency.

Very often, of course, journalists stir restlessly—at least some of them do—but in small ways with little avail, and then revert to the security and harmony of conformity and passivity. The system dominates; corporate consciousness and power win out again over the individual. Creativity begins to mean nothing more than "conforming more efficiently," or knowing the intricacies of the computer. Of course, there are rebels in this system—the existentialists—who rebel persistently, but they make little impact on the medium or the media system; many of them are "tolerated" for some reason, or they are ostracized from critical areas—or they are eliminated from the system altogether.

A Future-Oriented Liberalism

Existential journalism may be thought of as a kind of liberalism; certainly it is *future-oriented* and it is *freedom-loving*. With its emphasis on individualism, existentialism is liberalism of a kind, but certainly a liberalism with no belief in a natural social harmony and no hope for personal perfectibility. This is why an existential journalist is suspicious of organizations, groups, press councils, etc., along with professional ethical codes and sets of "responsibilities" for the press, designed to define or codify journalistic activities. This is a kind of liberalism that is opposed to the non-frictionalized and harmonized world of the communitarian or social engineer.

Not only do existential journalists think that journalists cannot be "perfected" by group-loyalty and ethics codes, but they actually prize the contentiousness, competitiveness, and pluralism that results from a lack of harmony both in journalistic enterprises and in society as a whole. So, it can be maintained that existential journalists, although very much liberals in some areas, also manifest many of the characteristics of the twentieth-century conservatives (or at least libertarians)—especially in their freedom-loving proclivities.

Perhaps the most thorough and satisfying development of existentialism in this century is contained in the writings of Karl Jaspers. He sees the main danger to the individual in our highly organized society as the growing desire to produce a standardized and conformist way of life for as many people as possible. He has discussed this problem in many of his works, but especially in his *Man in the Modern Age,* which is alluded to quite often in this book. The main way journalists can break out of this conformist philosophy is to embrace the existentialist commitment to freedom, choosing, and living beyond themselves. As Sartre has said in a famous passage from *Being and Nothingness,* "I am condemned to exist beyond my essence, beyond the causes and motives of my act. I am condemned to be free."

Lewis Mumford also emphasizes this necessity to strike out anew in continuous commitment; he writes in his *Transformations of Man* that "every goal man reaches provides a new starting point, and the sum of all man's days is just a beginning." Few journalists are living authentically in Sartre's freedom or cherishing Mumford's concept of constant future-plunging; journalists are settling for the comfort and rewards of conformity, of adjusting to the institutional system. The existentialist is faced with ever-increasing challenges to authentic living. The direction of society—and journalism—does, indeed, look dismal. This is no reason, however, to lose hope. It should rather be a stimulus to commitment, to living as fully and passionately as possible.

The coming generation of journalists can fall further into the stultifying comfort that journalistic institutionalization has fashioned for them, and with a hopeless or resigned sigh consign their very personhoods to unruffled conformity and stability. Or, they can join the decimated ranks of existential journalists, reaffirm their selfhood, commit themselves to enlarging the frontiers of freedom and authenticity, and rise to higher and higher levels of existence. The time is now. It is the only time we have.

2

Basic Journalistic Stances

I am a great believer in the device, practiced by most responsible American newspapers, of separating the news developments and the newspaper's editorial opinion. The first should be a flat, unembroidered account of the facts surrounding the items of news. It should be, so far as is humanly possible, free from the writer's or the commentator's personal interpretation or views.

—BARRY GOLDWATER, *The Conscience of a Majority*

Objectivity is not, as it is often implied in a false idea of "scientific" objectivity, synonymous with detachment, with absence of interest and care. How can one penetrate the veiling surface of things to their causes and relationship if one does not have an interest that is vital and sufficiently impelling for so laborious a task?

—ERICH FROMM, *Man for Himself*

THE TRAITS OR characteristics of journalists which help define their existential or non-existential natures are, of course, many and complex. They overlap in many cases and are otherwise difficult to isolate and discuss; but before getting into the main body of this work which discusses *existential journalism* in some detail, it might be well to deal briefly with journalistic stances or orientations which are most common today. Affecting the work of journalists today is a wide assortment of interests, ideologies, educational levels and cultural backgrounds, special talents, and so on. This is true even in societies where conformity and institutionalism have led to highly monolithic press systems.

It is certainly true in American society. The journalist in any society—but especially in a libertarian or quasi-libertarian society—is a many-sided person with several strong traits and tendencies. But even though all this is true, there seems to be in all journalists a basic and dominant psycho-ideological orientation which is either tilting in the direction of existentialism or away from existentialism. And it tends to manifest itself in most of the journalist's thinking and action.

Before getting more specifically into existential journalism *per se* in the following chapters, let us consider some of these basic stances which are found among journalists. One's orientation, undoubtedly, has a great deal to do with the kind of outlook one adopts as a journalist and even with stylistic characteristics of his journalism. In fact, his orientation affects his total journalistic *Weltanschauung*, for it leads him to consider certain fundamental issues related to journalism in ways consistent with this orientation. His basic stance indicates to a large degree his proclivity toward existentialism or against it. That is why it might be well to look at these stances here.

A journalist normally writes the way he thinks; he generally thinks according to his psycho-ideological orientation. A journalist, of course, may have mixture of orientations, but one will usually dominate. The problem comes when we attempt to classify orientations, but it can be done. And, although there are innumerable ways to set up such classification systems, the tendency is for all such systems to gravitate into two journalistic orientational types: (1) the mainly *objective* (scientific) journalist and (2) the mainly *subjective* (artistic) journalist. The second of these is to a large extent what I am referring to here as the *existential* journalist. This dichotomy will likely not satisfy everybody, but over the years while doing and teaching journalism, I have come to believe that these are the two main orientations or stances. It is not a matter always of "either-or"; rather it is a matter of dominant orientation, of a particular journalist being predominantly scientifically oriented or being predominantly artistically oriented. These two main tendencies will be taken up later in this chapter.

First, let us consider briefly several of the dualistic classifications into which basic orientations or stances may fall. Others are suggested in the figure ("Basic Journalistic Orientations") to be found later in the chapter.

Several Dichotomous Stances

One immediate problem with discussing stances is that there are so many dualistic classifications which can be used. There is, then, the problem of selection. And there is the more philo- sophical problem, emphasized in General Semantics, of the logical weakness of binary classifications: with such classifica- tions we are certain to do injustice to reality, for the "either-or" typology leads to distorted and simplistic thinking about the nature of the subject being classified. Naturally these are both formidable problems and each, in its own way, tends to distort reality. However, it must be noted that *any* system of classifica- tion (or of language usage in any form) distorts reality and is unsatisfactory in some sense. But in spite of the weaknesses of typologies, and the warnings of General Semanticists not- withstanding, I shall discuss journalistic orientations by "types"—with considerable emphasis given to dualistic gen- eralizations.

For me, a larger problem than the *semantic* weakness inher- ent in a binary classification is the problem of *selection* of these dualistic classifications. Journalists may be oriented primarily in dozens of ways which have approximate "opposites." What, then, are the most significant of these ways? This is the question which has haunted me, and it is quite possible that better classifications (more useful for analysis) could be used, but these which follow should at least serve as catalysts for disagreement even if they do not provide for everyone a personally satisfying method for understanding journalistic stances. And, it is my belief that in dealing with these several dualistic stances, there are some that are mainly *non-existential* and others that go together to coalesce into a rather clear *existential* orientation.

THE "INVOLVED" AND ALOOF STANCES

This is a very basic and common way of considering jour- nalists in binary fashion. The 'involved" journalist is generally considered one who is oriented to participating, to activism, to being personally and emotionally involved in the events of the day. He does not believe in neutrality for the journalist; he thinks it desirable that he bring his own ideological beliefs, preferences and biases to bear on his journalism. He is the person many refer to as the "activist" journalist who, as J. K. Hvistendahl says, "looks at traditional reporting as being sterile and . . . considers reporters who refuse to commit themselves to a point of view as being cynical or hypocritical."[1] Hvistendahl goes on to say that "truth-as-I-see it" reporting might be a more accurate description of this new trend in journalism than "activist reporting" for these "new" journalists believe that the reporter who is seeking the truth should report the truth *as they see it.* The *involved* journalist, as I prefer to call him here, desires to bring himself, his intelligence, his sensitivites, his judgments to bear on the news of the day; he is not satisfied to be a mere bystander, an objective observer, a recorder or a neutralist.

The journalist with the *aloof orientation*, on the other hand, maintains that journalism is primarily a disinterested activity where audiences should not be encumbered by the journalists' biases, prejudices, judgments, feelings and opinions. The journalist with the *aloof* orientation is often called the "objective" journalist (see Chapter 1), although this is probably a misnomer. But he does subscribe to the Neutralist Position whereby the journalist keeps himself and his opinions and judgments out of his journalism—or tries to. This is still a dominant orientation in the United States and is fostered in schools and departments of journalism—although it did have a shot of new vigor injected into it by subjectivists and activists during the 1960's. Much of this personalism still clings to large segments of the American press.[2]

THE "DIONYSIAN" AND "APOLLONIAN" STANCES

Another interesting and useful dualistic way to describe one's journalistic stance is to categorize him as either "Dionysian" or "Apollonian." These are the dichotomous tendencies toward emotion on one hand and toward reason on the other. This dualism was first highlighted in these terms by Nietzsche in *The Birth of Tragedy from the Spirit of Music.* He observed two opposite elements in Greek tragedies and believed them to be

---

[1] "The Reporter as Activist: Fourth Revolution in Journalism," *The Quill* (Feb. 1970), p. 8.

[2] The influence of such writers as Gay Talese, Gail Sheehy, Larry King, Willie Morris, Norman Mailer, Tom Wolfe, Truman Capote and Robert Daley were especially influential in the "New" journalism during the 1960's and into the 1970's.

basic metaphysical principles in reality. Nietzsche named them for two Greek gods—Apollo, the god of light, and Dionysus, the god of wine.

Dionysus can be thought of as a symbol for emotion, mysticism, a free and unfettered spirit, intuition, irrationality, and a kind of darkness. Apollo, on the other hand, is symbolic of reason, beauty, order, wisdom, and light.

Nietzsche, it seems, considered Apollo (Reason) a necessary element, but unreliable and thus an inferior guide to existence; in other words, he believed that such an orientation provides man an inadequate view of reality. In many ways, therefore, Nietzsche might be called the "Father of Existential Journalism." For Nietzsche the symbol of Dionysus is superior to that of Apollo, for Dionysus is the free spirit that offers man, through some kind of mysterious sensitivity or intuition, a more valid and profound vision of reality.

THE "POETIC" AND "PROSAIC" STANCES

A third dualistic classification of journalists might be constructed on the basis of their stylistic proclivities. Some journalists, of the Dionysian type discussed above, tend to subjectivize their journalism in an attempt to get beneath the surface of reality and present a fuller and more authentic picture. These are the *poetic* journalists. Other journalists, largely Apollonian, are content with the more traditional style of expression common among journalists who have adopted what might be termed "the wire-service" style.

This basic difference in communicative expression stems from the dominant orientation accepted by the journalists: poetic (a kind of "open" or flexible style) or prosaic (a kind of "closed" or mechanistic style). The Poetic Journalist is more personal or individual and less dogmatic in his style than is his counterpart. Also, he is more "impressionistic." He is willing to experiment with his journalism, especially in matters of story form and style. He is not as "hemmed in" by normal or traditional practices as is the more disciplined Prosaic Journalist. He is not very concerned about keeping himself out of his story; in fact he delights in giving his journalism the stamp of his own individual personality. He places great importance on his own ability to adapt his style to the story, and has great respect for self-expression, freedom, and autonomy.[3]

The *Prosaic Journalist*, on the other hand, is a believer in facts. He stresses literalness and explicit statements; he is interested in the accuracy of his stories—at least in the accuracy of what he selects to be in his stories. He praises what he calls "objectivity," considering it the same as reliability and truthfulness. The prosaic mind, according to George W. Morgan, considers the objective as identical with the factual. "In addition, and most important," Morgan writes, "it is believed that to be objective means to withhold the feelings and to be detached and impersonal."[4]

As Morgan rightly points out, facts are important to a person (and certainly to a journalist), but they can be overstressed to the detriment of other things which are equally important. For example, Morgan says that persons with "prosaic minds" tend to have little respect for interpretation "because it appears incompatible with fact: fact is what *is*, they think, while interpretation is whatever one makes it; facts are believed to be objective, and interpretation, subjective." Morgan notes that for prosaic persons, knowledge of facts—no matter how isolated, irrelevant or minuscule—becomes genuine knowledge and interpretation becomes prejudice; for the journalist with this orientation, "sticking to the facts" is the height of responsibility—anything else is "irresponsible fancy."[5]

THE "PERSONALIST" AND "FACTUALIST" STANCES

These orientations are quite similar to the poetic and prosaic discussed above except that they relate to the total outlook on journalism and its purpose, going beyond the simple *style* of the journalism. The Personalist is the "people-oriented" journalist who makes most decisions on the basis of the way he thinks they will affect *people*—including himself. His main concern is with

---

[3] For a discussion of "psychic openness" and other characteristics of the communication style of the Poetic Journalist, see Chapter 6 ("Style: The Dimension of Self") in A. Donald Bell and J. C. Merrill, *Dimensions of Christian Writing* (Grand Rapids, Mich.: Zondervan Publishing House, 1970).

[4] George W. Morgan, *The Human Predicament* (New York: Dell Publishing Co.—a Delta Book, 1970), p. 83.

[5] *Ibid.*, p. 88.

people, and he takes their feelings and sensitivities into consideration before he writes a story or gives it a certain emphasis in the news. People are always at the center of his journalism, and in an important way he is a utilitarian for he is thinking of consequences. In other words, the Personalist will be largely controlled by his sensitivity to people connected with the story; this is very much an "involved" or "subjective" stance and is at variance with what might be called *factualism*—or the orientation of dispassionate neutralism which focuses on *what* was said or done.[6]

The Factualist is one who is oriented toward journalistic aloofness or neutralism, taking a kind of prosaic position in his communication style. He concentrates on the facts, the events themselves, on what happened, on what people say, and the like. The *what* of the story is more important than the *why*—even if the *what* is simply an accurate accounting of somebody else's version of what happened, or somebody else's opinion. Although the Factualist is usually considered the "objective" journalist, having varying degrees of suspicion of, or hostility to, what he sees as involved, evaluative or subjective journalism. He tries diligently not to become involved in his story—or with the people of his story. His is the orientation of detachment, at least from personal opinions, attitudes or biases for self or for others so that his subjective feelings will not determine what he considers news or how he presents it. Facts to the Factualist are sacred; they are to be presented dispassionately and accurately, and if they are, the audience member should get the best possible picture of the total event, unadorned by the ideological and psychological biases of the reporter and editor.

THE "EXISTENTIAL" AND "RATIONAL" SUPER-STANCES

In a way, all the preceding orientations coalesce into either existential or rational emphases. The basic questions behind these stances seem to be: How involved and committed should journalists be? What is reality and how should journalists best get at it? And, finally, how should they pass on such "reality-

---

[6] For a more extended discussion of people-oriented and fact-oriented journalists, see J. C. Merrill and R. L. Lowenstein, *Media, Messages, and Men* (New York: David McKay, 1971), pp. 244-46.

information"? Earlier, the existential orientation was related to the Dionysian, and the rational orientation to the Apollonian. Just as easily, we might refer to the existential orientation as Romantic and the rational orientation as Platonic. It is basically the old conflict between Emotion (Intuition) and Reason (Logic). Also, we might connect the Artistic orientation with existential orientation, and the Prosaic (or Scientific) with the Rationalist.

At the risk of confusing the issue, we could further postulate that an *intellectual* orientation is closely related to existentialism. The term "intellectual," however, is enshrouded in more semantic fog than almost any term we could use, and it is difficult to speak of a journalist with an "intellectual" orientation. C. Wright Mills sees the intellectual journalist as somewhat akin to the existentialist because he has a tragic sense of life.[7] He realizes that grassroots democratic controls have become practically nonexistent—at least minimized—and that seemingly irresponsible actions by persons at the top are permitted—even encouraged—by The System. Others are dependent on the Leaders and must suffer the consequences of their ignorance and mistakes, their self-deceptions and their biased motives. It is the recognition of this that gives the Intellectual a sense of tragedy.

The intellectual journalist easily becomes frustrated, for too often he has gained the illusion that his thinking and concerns make a real difference in the affairs of society; he slowly wakes up to the fact that this is not really the case. But even though the Intellectual may have some characteristics in common with the existentialist, he is often quite different. For instance, the existentialist would fight harder than the Intellectual for freedom and autonomy; he would not "give up" as quickly. According to Mills, the intellectual person is a slave to somebody or some policy, and, although he may exercise a limited amount of freedom in his actions, he knows he must not go beyond these limits. He must ever watch his step. He must pull his punches to keep from offending his editor, his publisher, or some powerful person or group in his community. In many cases the intellectual journalist has adapted to these pressures, to these restricting forces, and has tried to confine his "creativity" and "individual-

---

[7] See C. Wright Mills, "The Social Role of the Intellectual," Ch. 3 in *Power, Politics and People* (New York: Ballentine Books, 1962). For another excellent discussion of this subject in relation to journalism, see Leo Rosten, "The Intellectual and the Mass Media," *Daedalus* (Spring, 1960), pp. 33-46.

ity" to compiling rationales for conformity and to formulating schemes for better (therefore more "responsible") collective action.

The Intellectual, of course, does not *have* to escape into a private or inauthentic world of his own; he can become existential; he can be committed; he can keep pushing, learning, discussing, writing and acting—tuning in to important dialogue everywhere. He does not need to cease caring, thinking, agitating, taking serious things seriously; but it is a temptation, for being a "thinker" he realizes the growing insignificance of the individual person and the deterministic tendencies of a mass society.

The existentialist position insists that the journalist involve himself, commit himself, ever moving, ever changing—in short, he must continue to make or create himself. "Man is nothing else but what he makes of himself," Sartre has said, calling this the first principle of existentialism.[8] Certainly the existential journalist, in the serious business of making himself, would not be devoid of rationality, nor would he be a complete foe of Reason. Again, it is a matter of emphasis: the existential journalist would stress intuition, feeling and any other aspect of subjectivism which might help him acquire a more complete and realistic picture of the event or personality he is describing.

Existentialism does not exclude rationalism, but it does give significant emphasis to emotional and intuitive concerns. It also gives extraordinary attention to personal freedom—including the freedom to react emotionally or instinctively to one's environment. As Hazel Barnes says, the existentialist's "one certainty is his own freedom."[9] The existentialist believes that one cannot be ethical in his actions unless he is free; ethics implies freedom. I *ought* implies I *can*—that I have a choice. Therefore, it is easy to see why existentialists believe that B. F. Skinner and other determinists are "beyond ethics" since they believe that people are enslaved to forces over which they have no control, forces which cause them to act in certain ways regardless of their desires.

The Rationalist, in contrast to the existentialist, has a ten-

---

[8] Jean-Paul Sartre, *Existentialism and Human Emotions* (New York: Philosophical Library, 1957), p. 15.

[9] *An Existentialist Ethics* (New York: Random House—Vintage Books, 1971), p. 51.

dency to be more the scientist than the artist, the prosaic man than the poet, the Platonist than the Romantic, the Apollonian than the Dionysian. William Barrett has compared him to Jonathan Swift's "Laputans" in *Gulliver's Travels*.[10] He would be one of the cerebral people, powerful but dreary, and scientifically oriented. And, as Barrett says, the whole Romantic movement was an attempt to escape from Laputa—a protest of feeling against reason. This Romantic protest was furthered by the early existentialists such as Kierkegaard, who maintained that "it was intelligence and nothing else that had to be opposed." But Kierkegaard did not disparage intelligence; in fact he speaks of it with great respect. But he did believe it needed opposition with all the resources and intelligence at his disosal. It is significant that Kierkegaard called himself the "subjective thinker."[11] It is this "subjective thinking"—a sort of harmonious marriage of emotion and intelligence—that marks the existentialist in journalism and differentiates him from the Rationalist in journalism who is determined to exclude judgment and emotion from his work and make his every decision—ethical and otherwise—on the basis of Reason, and Reason alone.

The Two Basic Journalistic Tendencies

Out of all the various stances discussed above, two basic journalistic tendencies emerge. One of these is what might be referred to as a "subjective" orientation or tendency and the other as an "objective" tendency. The first is a tendency toward involvement and the second is a tendency toward aloofness. The first is more "sense-oriented" and the second is more "fact-oriented." The journalist with the "objective" tendency might be said to be more scientific than the "subjectivist," who is more artistic.

Although every journalist is, indeed, schizophrenic to some degree in respect to these two tendencies, my experience with journalism students and practicing journalists for some twenty-five years convinces me that every person in journalism evidences significantly more of one of these tendencies than of the other. An interesting hypothesis presents itself—one which I

---

[10] William Barrett, *Irrational Man* (New York: A Doubleday Anchor Book, 1962), pp. 122-23.

[11] *Ibid.*, p. 150.

believe is valid, but which has never really been tested: that journalists with the aloof, scientific or disinterested orientation are those whose pre-journalism education and interests were more "prosaic" than "poetic," more "scientific" than "artistic." And, on the other hand, the so-called "subjective" or involved journalists are persons with a pre-journalism background showing an inclination toward imaginative literature, philosophy and the humanities generally. It is also probably true that the "subjectivists" are more emotional, more sensitive, more convinced of their own rightness, more desirous to proselytize and propagandize, and more dogmatic than are the so-called "objectivists" or uninvolved journalists.

If the two orientations were to be summarized in terms of the various dichotomous tendencies discussed earlier, here is the way each would look:

• *The Existential (involved or artistic) Stance*—romantic, poetic, Dionysian, mystical, intuitive, emotional, subjective, personal, informal, directive, persuasive, humanistic, judgmental, liberal.

• *The Rationalist (aloof or scientific) Stance*—neutralist, Platonist and Apollonian, prosaic, objectivist, impersonal, formal, reportive, disinterested, non-judgmental, calm, unemotional, conservative.

Institutionalized journalism, or what might be called "Establishment Journalism" in the United States, has championed the second of these basic tendencies. Journalism schools and departments give significantly more emphasis to it than to the more subjective orientation. The underground journalistic movement of the 1960's, coupled with the resurrection of subjective "New" journalism[12] by such writers as Wolfe, Mailer, and Capote, made a noticeable dent (at least temporarily) in the aloof or scientific orientation, but news media and programs in journalism education still give short shrift to judgmental, involved, intuitive journalistic subjectivism.

There is still an overriding conviction in journalism that reporters should keep their opinions and biases out of their

---

[12] An excellent discourse on "new journalism," readable and brief is a monograph, *The New Journalism: A Critical Perspective* (Association for Education in Journalism, 1974). One of the most stinging criticisms of "new" journalism is found (pp. 440-41) in John Tebbel, *The Media in America* (New York: New American Library Mentor Books, 1974).

Basic Journalistic Orientations

Existentialist Stance	Rationalist Stance
Involved	Aloof
Romantic	Realistic
Poetic	Prosaic
Artistic	Scientific
Subjective	Objective
Personal	Impersonal
Passionate	Dispassionate
Informal	Formal
Directive	Imitative
Warm	Cold
Opinionated	Non-opinionated
Judgmental	Non-judgmental
Liberal	Conservative
Committed	Neutral
Dionysian	Apollonian
Intuitive	Logical
Personalistic	Factualistic
Non-conformist	Conformist
Unpredictable	Predictable
Flexible	Standardized

Values	Values
Freedom	Responsibility
Instability	Stability
Pluralism	Monism
Diversity	Sameness
Experimentation	Consistency
Change	Changelessness
Future	Past/Present
Spontaneity	Predictability
Egoism	Altruism
Individualism	Collectivism
Creativity	Conformity
Self-reliance	Dependence
Autonomy	Institutionalism
Emotions	Reason
Will	Determinism
Rebellion	Conformity

stories and that subjective pieces and commentary be separated from news stories and be clearly identified. Those who are in favor of "integrated" journalism—in the sense of combining the reporter's judgments and opinions with the verifiable facts—are very much in the minority and are felt to be the eccentrics of modern American journalism. More about this will be presented later (in Chapter 5).

In spite of this "objectivist" leaning in American journalism, various existentialist voices do caution against it. Karl Jaspers notes that we need a great dissatisfaction "with what is merely correct," and that truth is "infinitely *more* than scientific correctness."[13] Hwa Yol Jung states that "the affirmation of objectivism to the exclusion of subjectivity is misleading because it ignores the place of subjectivity in thought and observation."[14] He continues:

> What is observable (a datum), for example, is always related to the awareness of an observer. A datum of observation is not yet a fact, and a fact is meaningful only in relation to the observer for whom it is a fact. Thus a fact is nothing but meaning given to a datum (or data) by the observer in the process of observation. Further, the truth of a fact or thought for one observer is sanctioned intersubjectively—that is, by a scientific or intellectual community. As consciousness is intentional, reflective thought, whether philosophical or scientific, is neither entirely subjective nor entirely objective.

Back in the 1940's the noted journalist, H. L. Mencken, put it more bluntly: "We talk of objective reporting. There is no such thing. I have been a reporter for many years, and I can tell you that no reporter worth a hoot ever wrote a purely objective story. You get a point of view in it. . . . You can't escape it. A man that is worth reading at all has opinions. He has ideas. And you are not going to improve him by trying to choke him."[15]

Journalism has been largely one-dimensional for many years. Even in more advanced countries journalism has been thought to be pretty simple: just give the facts in order of their importance.

---

[13]"Existenzphilosophie" in Walter Kaufmann (ed.), *Existentialism from Dostoevsky to Sartre* (New York: New American Library—Meridian Books, 1975), p. 175.

[14] In Hwa Yol Jung (ed.), *Existential Phenomenology and Political Theory: A Reader* (Chicago: Henry Regnery Co., 1972), xxvi.

[15] In Theo Lippman, Jr. (ed.), *A Gang of Pecksniffs* (New Rochelle, NY.: Arlington House, 1975), p. 203.

Oversimplifcation is, to a great extent, still the rule. The journalist has, at least in the United States, been conceived of as somebody who, either because of an ability or desire to write or a penchant for prying open doors of secrecy, gravitated to a journalistic position. Or, he was a political agitator who landed in journalism instead of politics. Generally, the journalist has been an uninvolved, reportorial type who has been nurtured in an atmosphere of the "objective" school of journalism which prizes the neutral stance. Occasionally, however, a Tom Wicker or a Daniel Schorr will break through—evidencing an existential emphasis. But this does not happen very often, and when it does even the "professional colleagues" tend to make such a stance uncomfortable.

What are the main characteristics of the "existential journalist" and how can he function in today's highly institutionalized and professionalized journalism? The broad outlines of this existential journalism is the subject of the next chapter.

3

Existential Journalism: Outlines

The journalist . . . can merge himself in the tension and the reality of the day. . . . He can seek out that innermost region where the soul of the age takes a step forward. He deliberately interweaves his destiny with that of the epoch. He takes alarm, he suffers, and he balks when he encounters Nothingness. He becomes insincere when he is content with that which brings satisfaction to the majority. He soars towards the heights when he sincerely fulfills his being in the present.

—KARL JASPERS, *Man in the Modern Age*

The press must be a vital participant in public affairs, and an open and bold participant . . . unashamed of the fact that it is accepting a responsibility for playing such a role. . . . and it must not depend on the safe and stifling rules of some false objectivity, but depend upon the talent, the knowledge, the experience, the courage, and, above all, the individuality of the people who work in the press.

—TOM WICKER, *The Quill*

EXISTENTIAL JOURNALISM is a kind of synthesis of the attitudes expressed above in the quotations from a philosopher and a journalist. Unfortunately, the term is too often denuded of its vital meaning by being considered, when it is considered at all, as something nearly synonymous with "New Journalism." Actually it is different; for it is not simply an attitude or stance of rebellion for rebellion's sake, nor is it an obsession with writing style or form, nor is it a concern for exhaustive communication. Rather, existential journalism is that aspect of journalism mainly manifested in an attitude of freedom, commitment, rebellion, and responsibility. It makes no *a priori* assumptions as to the direction the journalism should take. It is mainly an orientation of being "true to one's self," however trite this may sound. So we can say that existential journalism is not the same as New Journalism, although they do have certain characteristics in common.

New Journalism, in its generalized meaning, is mainly concerned with form and style—or with an anti-establishment bias predominantly, or with confronting public taste through the use of four-letter words and unorthodox ideas, subjects, and pictures. It does often resemble existential journalism in that there is an inclination to rebel against conformity and authoritarian tendencies. However, it has been my observation that the so-called "New Journalists" are mainly "literary figures" who want a continuous forum, or they are counter-culture types who desire to shock the sensitivities of the general public. Often they are not really authentic and individualistic: they conform to their "own crowd" and the dictates of "their" philosophy or ideology; they do what seems to be currently in vogue with the rebels. In a sense, their guiding motto seems to be "Nonconformists of the World, Unite!" This is definitely *not* the stance of the existential journalist.

Some General Characteristics

Existential journalism is mainly a *subjective* journalism—subjective in the sense that it puts special stress on the *person* of the journalist himself. Certainly, I am not talking of an extreme subjectivism; rather the kind of existential journalism that is realistic and meaningful is a modified subjective journalism. It is mainly subjective, personal, and passionate; but at the same time it has a firm foundation of reasonableness. And, of course, reasonableness impinges on journalistic freedom, limiting it by *self*-assertion, making it "responsible" freedom. Therefore, when I use the term *existential* journalism, I am referring to this modified or nonextreme journalistic stance of existentialism.

In journalism, we normally repress the sense of subjectivity. We fail to recognize its inevitability as well as its pitfalls, its mystery, and its sober source of strength. Man is subjective. He cannot escape from himself—nor should he attempt it. When he tries to be objective—a "reflector" of his environment—he takes on a false nature; he becomes inauthentic. Freud has said that a person has an unconscious that motivates and influences his conscious choice of words and messages. The existentialist in journalism would agree with this, but it does indeed pose the problem of a kind of neutralist objectivity. Erich Fromm insists that "objectivity does not mean detachment, it means respect; that is, the ability not to distort and to falsify things, persons, and oneself."[1] Very often the journalist will adopt a stance of detachment, of disinterest; he is attempting to be true to what he calls "objectivity." Fromm takes issue with such a stance, and says that the idea that "lack of interest is a condition for recognizing the truth is fallacious."[2]

Existentialism is a philosophy of the subject rather than of the object; this, of course, shifts the emphasis for the existential journalist from an obsession with the "thing" or "person" he is writing about to his (the writer's) *perception* of what is being reported. The subject is the initiator of action and the center of feeling: this *subject* is the journalist. John Macquarrie points out that often such a style of philosophizing appears to be anti-intellectualist. The existentialist thinks passionately, Macquarrie says, "as one who is involved in the actualities of existence." Probably the existentialist who took an extreme position in favor of "feeling" *vis-à-vis* "the rational man" was Miguel de Unamuno. Even though some other existentialists have paid more respect (especially Karl Jaspers) to reason than did Unamuno, it is still true that they all claim to found their philosophy on a broad non-rational basis and eschew any narrow intellectualism.[3]

Jean Wahl in his 1949 brief discussion of existentialism defines the existent individual (drawing on Kierkegaard) as one (a) who has an infinite interest in himself and his destiny, (b) always feels himself to be in the process of becoming, with a task before him, and (c) is impassioned, is inspired with what Kierkegaard calls "the passion of freedom."[4] Wahl also quotes

---

[1] Erich Fromm, *Man for Himself* (Greenwich, Conn.: A Fawcett Premier Book, 1966), p. 111.

[2] *Ibid.*, A good discussion of this point can be found in Karl Mannheim, *Ideology and Utopia* (New York: Harcourt, Brace and Co., 1936).

[3] John Macquarrie, *Existentialism* (Baltimore: Penguin Books, Inc., 1973), pp. 2-3.

[4] Jean Wahl, *A Short History of Existentialism* (New York: Philosophical Library, 1949), p. 4.

Heidegger as insisting that a person must constantly be moving upward and forward ("transcending Nothingness") towards (1) the world, (2) other persons, and (3) the future. "Therefore," he writes, "each of us is always in front of himself . . . constantly oriented toward his possibilities."[5] Increasingly, according to Heidegger, persons are living at the inauthentic level of Being; this, he says, is largely due to mass society "in which individuals are prepared to lead average and secure lives, left without major decisions, undisturbed and even protected by society in return for their specific services and functions predetermined by the managers of mass society."[6]

Existential journalism is future-oriented journalism. The existential journalist looks ever ahead, even when he writes of past (and "so-called present") events. In so looking, he takes upon himself what William Barrett has called "the burden of the past (or of what out of the past he selects as his inheritance)" and thereby "orients himself in a certain way to his present and actual situation in life."[7]

Existentialists make much of the thesis that existence precedes essence; in other words, a person makes himself what he is; his individual essence or nature develops out of his existence. He has no fixed essence handed him at birth; rather, he fabricates his own nature out of his freedom and the historical situation in which he lives. So, he must be future-oriented; he must project himself forward, using his freedom to make decisions and to live authentically. Sartre puts the idea in these words: "We mean that man first of all exists, encounters himself, surges up in the world—and defines himself afterwards." Sartre continues in his essay, "Existentialism is a Humanism," to say that man is really indefinable, and this is because to begin with he is nothing. "He will not be anything," Sartre states, "until later, and then he will be what he makes of himself."[8]

Rollo May has provided a brief and succinct statement on the character and importance of existentialism. This quotation, I think, provides the main foundation of existentialism upon which a philosophy of journalism can be built:

---

[5] *Ibid.*, p. 16.

[6] Hanno Hardt, "The Dilemma of Mass Communication: An Existential Point of View," *Philosophy & Rhetoric* (Penn State University), Vol. 5, No. 3.

[7] *Irrational Man: A Study in Existential Philosophy* (New York: Doubleday Anchor Books, 1962), p. 228.

[8] Quoted in Macquarrie, *op. cit.*, p. 3.

The protest of the existentialists was violent and at times desperate (as in Nietzsche), at other times noble and courageous (as in the resistance movement of Camus and Sartre), even if it seemed to many observers to be ineffectual against the on-moving lava of conformity, collectivism, and the robot man. The existentialists' central proclamation was this: No matter how great the forces victimizing the human being, man has the capacity to *know* that he is being victimized, and thus to influence in some way how he will relate *to* his fate. There is never lost that kernel of the power to take some stand, to make some decision, no matter how minute. This is why the existentialists hold that man's existence consists, in the last analysis, of his freedom. Tillich has phrased this view beautifully, "Man becomes truly human only at the moment of decision."[9]

Taking into consideration the general principles of existentialism summarized above, I think we can say that existential journalism:

- emphasizes that the existential journalist is a free and authentic person, not simply a cog in the impersonal wheel of journalism; that he is not replaceable or expendable;
- brings into sharp relief the uniqueness of every journalist's individual existence and personality;
- causes practitioners to develop their integrity and individual personalities and to project their personalities into society through their journalism;
- makes them rebel against being lost, anonymous functionaries in journalism;
- extols freedom and responsibility for decisions in a day when more and more people are trying to escape freedom and journalists are ever more cheerfully disappearing into the recesses of highly institutionalized "corporate" journalism. (The existential journalist may rebel against this trend toward corporate journalism, but he is in for a hard fight, for the growth of totalitarian regimes and the steady drift toward collective, paternalistic societies is testimony to the desire to "escape from freedom" which Erich Fromm has written about so perceptively.)

Also, we can say that the existential journalist wants to practice a journalism that means that he:

1) takes a certain viewpoint, a certain position, a certain

---

[9] As quoted in Raymond Van Over (ed.), *The Psychology of Freedom* (Greenwich, Conn.: Fawcett Premier Books, 1974), p. 344.

stand, and ceases what may be called the "objective-neutralism" fallacy;

2) considers alternatives of action and makes a commitment to one or some, not resting on the comfortable assumption that a little of everything ranged rather equally is the best, the fairest, truest, and most objective journalism;

3) makes no hestitation in choosing, selecting, making decisions as to editorial determinations; the journalist insists on persistent choices, hard ones as well as easy ones. (The journalist knows that in a very true sense in journalism *when he chooses for himself, he chooses for all*. He, in effect, universalizes his choices; he determines for all what is "news" for him. He structures the world for others while structuring his own world in words and pictures.)

4) considers consequences of journalistic action and takes responsibility for it, not "passing the buck" or "copping out" by offering excuses or saying that he is simply following orders of a superior. (For the existential journalist there is no "superior" so far as decision-making or ethical stand is concerned. The journalist *is his own standard*; there is no other.)

5) accepts and *uses* freedom—personal and journalistic. He is dedicated to freedom; it is his imperative, and as an existentialist he sees *his* freedom as everyone's. He chooses freedom and, in so doing, he chooses freedom as desirable for everyone, thus adding a kind of Kantian dimension to his journalistic foundation. What he wills for himself, he wills for everyone. And in the case of freedom, this is a highly dangerous and often uncomfortable position since the freedom of others may often cause actions not in keeping with one's own values or interests.

6) is vital, dynamic, passionate, and committed. (The existential journalist is repelled by stagnant, conformist, routine, uncommitted, dispassionate journalism—journalism that enshrines harmony, stability, safety, and complacency. The existential journalist wants to practice vigorous, dangerous journalism. It is through such a practice that he really *exists* as a journalist; thus he makes himself constantly into a journalist who is authentic; it is in this way that he creates his own journalistic essence, that he becomes more than a piece of machinery in the newsroom.)

7) extols individualism. (This means that he looks on the world and journalistic issues from *his* personal viewpoint. It means that how he looks on the world as a reporter *is* the world;

and as a reporter he transmits at least a portion of his total perceptions to his reader as *his world.)*

Freedom: The Existentialist's Imperative

What a journalist does in specific cases does not matter as much as the fact that he *does something.* The supreme virtue for the existentialist is probably the most old-fashioned of all: *integrity.* And a person cannot have integrity unless he utilizes his capacity to choose, to act, to make decisions. Basic to man is this act of choosing; the existentialist sees man's very nature consisting of choosing. And this choosing is an outgrowth of freedom; or, said another way, it can have real meaning only in an atmosphere of freedom. To the question, "What good is life?" comes the answer: Life in the abstract is worthless. As a person lives his life, its value can be judged by what he puts into it. Values are a projection of man's personal freedom. For the existentialist man *is* freedom; he does not possess freedom. Freedom, for the existentialist, comes as close as possible to constituting man's very essence. Man's most basic desire is for independent, free choice—at least, this is *existential* man's most basic desire.

Responsibility, for the existentialist, is seen as freedom's anchorage. Man is responsible for himself, of course, but also for each act, and for the consequences of each act. Nobody else can be responsible for what a person is; each person must act freely and accept the responsibility for his action. And to choose for oneself is to choose for others. What would others do in my place? Strangely, perhaps, existentialists view this universalized personal choice in much the same way as the coldly formal Kant did: You must never will what you cannot consistently will should be willed by other rational (i.e., free and responsible) beings. This heavy sense of personal responsibility the existentialists call "anguish." Sartre has said that man is "condemned" to be free, and Kierkegaard wrote of the necessity to choose only "in fear and trembling." But choose we must—for ourselves and for all others, with no final assurance that our choice is the "right" one.[10]

---

[10] Abraham Kaplan, *The New World of Philosophy* (New York: Vintage Books, 1961), pp. 97-128.

Naturally we attempt to escape the implications of this existential situation. Lama Anagarika Govinda has written that "generally we live away from life, either by being occupied with the past, or by anticipating the future."[11] Only while living "in the present, i.e., in moments of full awareness and 'awakedness,' are we free," she added.[12] Often we try to escape our present— and thus ourselves; we try to deny that we are responsible for our actions by denying that we are free. This is "bad faith." The journalist, for example, may often say that *he* would not have written the story in such a way—or would not have written it at all—but that he "had to do it" because he was told by his editor. He is thereby denying his freedom and refusing to accept personal responsibility for his actions. In practical terms, this embrace of "determinism" in various of its forms, amounts to denying that we are to blame for our actions—or for our morality. Existentialists, enshrining freedom, have no sympathy for these deterministic philosophies. And people who accept them, who try to escape the human condition of freedom and personal responsibility, are seen as cowards. The existentialist realizes that man must accept unquestioned responsibility for his ethical choices and actions. Man is an individualist: he is the end-all and the be-all of values. If the journalist is free he is, in a sense, condemned to live with his freedom—condemned to live with uncertainty and shifting situations in which he must constantly fashion his own standards. This is a terrifying, uncertain experience, filled with anguish; but it is the key to authentic essence-building existence.

Self-deception, for the existentialist, is the greatest vice, for it robs man of his personhood, his integrity; it deludes him into thinking that he is nothing more than a robot having an essence pushed upon him by *outside* forces. Man *makes himself*, says the existentialist, or defines what he is in the course of choosing, acting and existing.

The philosophical strain of freedom is basic to a sound and authentic journalistic orientation. Existentialism stresses this freedom; so does Kant, actually, but there is a difference. Sartre agrees with Kant in conceiving of freedom as "desiring both itself and the freedom of others." But, Sartre notes, Kant believes

---

[11] Quoted in Van Over (ed.), *The Psychology of Freedom*, p. 248.
[12] *Ibid.*, p. 249.

that "the formal and universal are enough to constitute an ethics"; existentialists, on the other hand, "think that principles which are too abstract run aground in trying to decide action."[13] Sartre emphasizes personal responsibility—absolute responsibility for actions taken in specific cases and considering specific circumstances. So we can say that the existentialist, although prizing freedom, is basically a situationist while Kant is a universalist.

Action implies freedom. Since existentialists advocate action, they would, of course, place freedom near to the heart of their philosophy. They have a passion for freedom; this is true of all varieties of existentialists. Freedom for the existentialist is a basic postulate for action; it is already present as a condition for human existence. Freedom, of course, is dangerous; it even tends to contain in itself the seed of its own destruction. Nikolai Berdyaev, an existentialist who has written much on the subject of freedom, puts it this way: "The tragedy of the world process is that of freedom; it is born of the inner dynamic of freedom, of its capacity for changing into its opposite."[14] In striking this note, Berdyaev is consistent with many of his fellow existentialists. Plato, although not an existentialist, had, in his classic "Paradox of Freedom," pre-dated the existentialists in pointing out this danger centuries earlier when he noted that free men could freely decide to become enslaved.

Freedom may indeed be dangerous. And for many it is uncomfortable; they constantly attempt to escape from it and live inauthentic lives—"in bad faith." Nevertheless, freedom is absolutely necessary to an open society, to a democracy, to a libertarian people—and certainly to a pluralistic and diversified journalism. And, as existentialists contend, there is no human dignity without freedom—and "the risk of increasing freedom must constantly be taken," as John Macquarrie puts it.[15] Existentialists generally link freedom with creativity. Without freedom *from* restraints, man cannot have freedom *for* creative activity. Berdyaev and other existentialists reveal a certain elitist or aristocratic tendency; the masses, they say, do not really value freedom and are satisfied with the routine daily existence. For this reason

---

[13] Jean-Paul Sartre, *Existentialism and Human Emotions* (New York: Philosophical Library—The Wisdom Library, 1957), p. 47.

[14] Macquarrie, *op. cit.*, p. 140.

[15] *Ibid.*, p. 141.

the masses "are peculiarly exposed to the dangers of dictator-ship, founded on demagogy."[16] This is undoubtedly true, for it is the rebel against the tryannizing and conforming influences of the masses who cherishes freedom; it is he who protests against every attempt to diminish freedom. It is he who realizes, as did Albert Camus, that "freedom preserves the power to protest and guarantees human communication."[17]

The freedom-loving journalist can find perhaps his greatest support from the existentialists, for here is a philosophy which rebels against any social control system which tends to enslave the individual human being and to lead to his depersonalization. Frederick Patka writes that existentialists "protest against this total subjection of the individual by the organized many" and that they "demand a bold revolt against this state of affairs with a view to the emancipation and autonomy of the individual per-son."[18]

The modern journalist, within whom the potent existentialist freedom is strong, will recognize the potential danger of manipu-lating and enslaving others. If he desires freedom for himself, he will desire it for others and he will cherish their authenticity and autonomy as he cherishes his own. The real freedom-lover, in other words, will defend freedom for others as well as for himself. He knows full well that when only *some* have freedom, they are tyrants and autocrats—or at least they have the potential within them to be. When *all* have freedom, at least everyone has the power to counteract tyranny and autocracy—or to escape from it through his own freedom. The existential journalist is certainly free to exercise his freedom in ways considered irre-sponsible to others, but the strain of Kantian morality and the humanist in him will temper his activities with moderation, concern, and *self*-responsibility and will keep him from falling into the abyss of nihilism.

The existential spirit is especially important for the journalist for it provides the fundamental foundation of his creative activ-ity; it spurs him to action, to commitment and a determination to launch out into new journalistic regions. What he *does* makes

---

[16] *Ibid.*

[17] Albert Camus, *The Rebel* (New York: Alfred Knopf, Inc. and Random House—Vintage Books, 1954), p. 291.

[18] Frederick Patka in F. Patka (ed.), *Existentialist Thinkers and Thought* (New York: The Citadel Press, 1966), pp. 42-43.

him authentic, real, human. How he reacts to his world through his journalism defines him as a journalist. *"Respondeo, ergo sum."*[19]

Journalists must respond to their environment—to their own journalistic situation. They are more than neutral observers; if they are not, then they are *nothing*. The true existentialist in journalism gets *into* the story, becomes part of the story. His perceptions, his sensitivity to the stimuli of the story infiltrates the story; in short, the existential journalist is part of the story and the story is part of him. This, of course, affects the journalistic Self and disrupts any demeanor of "objective neutralism"; it brings subjectivity to bear on the Event-Reporter-Report nexus, and it is what largely injects journalism with Dionysian ingredients of artistry, sensitivity, emotionalism, personalism, mysticism, opinionism, and creativity.

The Existential Journalist

Tom Wicker is one journalist on the contemporary scene who has challenged the news media to analyze themselves and get rid of the old notions of "objectivity" and "noninvolvement" which have all but been considered sacred in this century. The associate editor of *The New York Times* told a journalism group in 1975 that he saw the possibility for a "new age of the press" in America, a press which he characterized as "intellectual in the fundamental direction . . . challenging to all institutions of power . . . analytical in its general approach . . . involved in what is happening in our country."[20]

Since there are not many Wickers around today, it is good to have his hopeful words, indicating that existential journalism may be just around the corner. While I admire Wicker and applaud the substance of his optimism, I expect that it reflects mainly his "hopes" and the natural rhetoric of a person talking to journalists at a conference. If pessimism is characteristic of an existentialist, then, at least in this one respect, I am more existential than is Wicker. I do not see this American journalism in which the journalist will be "an open and bold participant" as

---

[19] See Ch. 12 ("Respondeo ergo Sum") in F. H. Heinemann, *Existentialism and the Modern Predicament* (New York: Harper Torchbooks, 1958), pp. 190-204.

[20] "Let's stop playing it safe," *The Quill* (December, 1975), p. 15.

imminent—or even possible in the long-run in this country. Timidity in journalism is being born; conformity and complacency are just now settling in. Increasing pressures from minority groups, government, the legal profession, and even from cautious and weak-kneed journalists themselves are killing any upsurge of existential journalism.

Journalism history can point to Addison, Steele, and Swift; it can single out Thomas Paine and Henry Thoreau; it can make a gesture toward I. F. Stone and Hodding Carter; and it can nod casually at Ernest Hemingway and H. L. Mencken; it can point to European "literary" journalists such as J.-P. Sartre and Albert Camus, and it can cast a cautious reference to Dan Rather, Tom Wicker, and Daniel Schorr. Journalism history can, indeed, dredge up some notable examples of existential journalists—but not very many.

Now, this is not to say that there have not been very many. But, generally, they are not the "big names" that burst forth into history or the public view; they are the pushers, tuggers, rebels, and involvers that go about their daily existential labors without benefit of national forum in the big newspapers, magazines, or broadcasting networks. A close study of the daily journalistic endeavors of individual journalists in the country would undoubtedly uncover a considerable number of existentialists. But they are not the wave of the future; in fact, there is no doubt but that they are being penalized at present, and in the future they will have no status or state in the increasingly timid, conformist, and corporate journalism.

A good example (perhaps the best) of an existential journalist is Albert Camus, who died in 1960. In 1943 he joined the underground group called "Combat," struggling against Nazi occupation of France. For this group, Camus edited a newspaper called *Combat*. The hundreds of articles he wrote for this paper make a record of the reactions of this sensitive, intelligent, and combative individual and provide an extended profile of an existentialist in journalism. During the black days of World War II, *Combat* was, for thousands of Frenchmen, a source of information, of stimulation, of pride, of hope and comfort. After the liberation of Paris (August, 1944), Camus continued his association with journalism by writing regularly for the weekly serious paper of Paris, *L'Express* (now a magazine). He also contributed articles to many French newspapers, doing so until the time of his death in an automobile accident in 1960.

Camus defined a good journalist as one who had a passionate concern and respect for himself, for others, and for truth. He believed that a good journalist was one "who, first of all, is supposed to have ideas."[21] In addition, Camus believed that the good journalist's task "is to inform the public on events which have just taken place," since "he is a sort of day-to-day historian whose prime concern is the truth." He elaborated on this, however, by saying that the "first news" is not always the best news and that "it is better to come in second and report the truth than to be first and false."[22]

Camus evidenced in his journalism (and in his novels and short stories) a depth and maturity indicative of existentialism. He treasured the rebel, to be sure, but he realized that freedom and rebellion implies responsibility. Maturity demands realism, and for Camus, realism led to the virtues of moderation. It was his belief that every individual must seek the measure, the harmony, the order, which will ensure his own freedom and integrity, and—equally important—the freedom and integrity of all others.

Without a doubt Camus was an existential journalist; he was other things, too, of course, but the *journalist* was very strong in him. But, in spite of this fact, Camus did not have much faith in journalism generally, considering it to be, by and large, superficial, careless, pedestrian, and vulgar. He seemed to realize that most journalists were non-existential, that they had no real desire to dig deeply into reality, to commit themselves to truth, to take unpopular positions, and to fight against the enslavements of mass society. In short, Camus saw the press situation as dismal. So had José Ortega y Gasset, the notable Spanish philosopher, who, too, had dabbled in journalism from time to time.

Ortega has referred to the "emanations of the press" as being on a "very low spiritual plane."[23] He calls the typical journalist

---

[21] Jean Daniel, "Camus as Journalist," *New Republic* (June 13, 1964), p. 19. For further details on Camus as a journalist, see Germaine Brée, *Camus and Sartre: Crisis and Commitment* (New York: Dell Publishing Co.—A Delta Book, 1972), pp. 36, 52, 203, 214, 245, and 249.

[22] Daniel, *op. cit.*

[23] *Mission of the University* (New York: W. W. Norton & Co.,—The Norton Library, 1944), p. 90.

"one of the least cultured types in contemporary society," and one that deforms reality when he "reduces the present to the momentary, and the momentary to the sensational."[24] It is obvious that Ortega did not think too highly of journalism, although its role in society was considered to be very important.

Karl Jaspers, too, was of somewhat the same mind about journalism. While recognizing the importance of the press in bringing "into the consciousness of the times what otherwise would remain the ineffective possession of a few individuals,"[25] he admits that it is extremely difficult to find a "terse and highly polished insight . . . amid the multifarious rubbish of what is printed from day to day."[26]

One of today's broadcast journalism reporters, Charles Kuralt, believes a great segment of news is being overlooked by the press. "There is much in our country to be confident and reassured about," he says, "but confidence and reassurance are not the province of the front page or the evening news."[27] Kuralt suggests that journalists could do more than merely inform people; "We may help educate them occasionally," he writes. "We may help broaden their vision and elevate their spirits. We may accept the responsibility we have to be better than we are, broader than we are, calmer and more reflective."[28] Jacques Ellul, a contemporary sociologist and social philosopher, agrees with Kuralt on his general view of journalism, saying that "the news is only about trouble, danger and problems."[29] This, he believes, is largely responsible for the anxiety that plagues individuals in today's society; he writes that

> . . . this gives man the notion that he lives in a terrible and frightening era, that he lives amid catastrophes in a world where everything threatens his safety. Man cannot stand this; he cannot live in an absurd and incoherent world (for this he would have to be heroic, and even Camus, who considered this the only honest posture, was not really able to stick to it); nor can he accept the idea that the problems, which sprout all around him, cannot be

---

[24] *Ibid.*

[25] Karl Jaspers, *Man in the Modern Age* (Garden City, N.Y.: Doubleday Anchor Books, 1957), p. 134.

[26] *Ibid.*, pp. 124-25.

[27] "Journalism is crisis-ridden; the country is not," *The Bulletin* of ASNE (Jan., 1976), p. 15.

[28] *Ibid.*

[29] Jacques Ellul, *Propaganda* (New York: Vintage Books, 1973), p. 146.

solved, or that he himself has no value as an individual and is subject to the turn of events. The man who keeps himself informed needs a framework in which all this information can be put in order; he needs explanations and comprehensive answers to general problems; he needs coherence. And he needs an affirmation of his own worth.

And then there is John Carroll, writing in New York's *The Village Voice* and criticizing the press coverage of Patty Hearst, before and during her trial:

> And so the crowds, the believers and the criers, the jailhouse johnnies and the electronic groupies fulfilled the media prophecy. They saw themselves in the funhouse media mirror. And they waved their arms at their own reflections, seeking fame by association, dancing jerkily on the outskirts of history. They came because the media said it was a big story; the media proved that it was a big story because the crowds came. It's like the old Gertrude Stein drinking song, "We're here because we're here because we're here because . . ."[30]

Now, back to Tom Wicker. He is one of my candidates for an outstanding existential journalist, but there are not many. He, too, attacks the press—but his stress is on the impulse of the press "to play it safe." Writing about the press and the Watergate Affair, Wicker says: "We'll never know how many things might have appeared, should have appeared, but did not appear because of that impulse of self-censorship on the part of the press, an impulse to play it safe."[31] According to Wicker, this tendency poses a great danger in journalism—perhaps the greatest—and editors, publishers, and reporters must constantly fight against it "with the greatest degree of alertness."[32] Wicker has consistently called for an existential stance in journalism; and his words have been clearer and more forceful in this regard than most journalists are prepared to accept.

It was to be expected that Wicker would be admonished for his existential position. An example of this was a letter in *The Quill* two months later,[33] most of which is quoted below:

---

[30] As reprinted in *The Bulletin* of ASNE (Jan., 1976), p. 15.

[31] *The Quill* (Dec. 1975), p. 16.

[32] *Ibid.*

[33] *The Quill* (Feb., 1976), p.4. The writer of the letter was B. R. Berry of Westerville, Ohio. His reaction probably reflects the opinion of the great majority of American journalists and journalism professors.

Wicker is suggesting the public be fed news oriented to advocate a particular point of view: "The press must above all be fair and accurate, but not necessarily be a press that is in the traditional sense of the word, objective and neurtral." The press as he sees it, would not depend greatly upon "the safe and stifling rules of some false objectivity, but depend upon the talent, knowledge, experience, courage, and above all, the individuality of the people who work in the press."

Do you really want the news people you know (or any other group for that matter) to have that much power and that little accountability? Such a position certainly is not in agreement with the new code of ethics just adopted by the American Society of Newspaper Editors. . . .

Wicker is afraid of playing it safe. I am afraid of irresponsibility. It can kill freedom of the press. There is no need for freedom of the press if it does not report the unbiased truth. Otherwise, we simply substitute one tyranny for another.

In February, 1976, Tom Wicker went out on a limb again—this time when he defended Daniel Schorr of CBS News. Not many other journalists of national reputation came to Schorr's defense; in fact, most were highly critical of the CBS reporter who made a copy of the House Intelligence Committee's report available for publication in *The Village Voice*, a New York weekly newspaper. CBS News had just suspended Schorr from his reporting duties for the action. Wicker was angry, and dealt with the subject in his column, syndicated by the New York Times Service and printed during the month by many newspapers. He began by saying that CBS News "had succumbed to a campaign launched within the Ford administration picturing the Central Intelligence Agency as an erring but basically worthy victim of those who leak its vital secrets and reporters who print them." Then he went on to give the history of the incident, and to relate it to the government charge about publication of the Pentagon Papers in 1971.

Wicker pointed a critical finger at the House of Representatives, and asked: "How is it different for the House to vote to suppress a public document than for a president to suppress it? If President Ford, for example, had decided not to make public the report of the Rockefeller Commission he appointed to study CIA abuses, would that have made it 'just plain wrong' for a good reporter like Dan Schorr to get hold of it and put it on the public record? Of course not." And, Wicker ended his column with a word of praise for Schorr: "After a year-long investigation conducted at public expense, it [the committee report] was in fact a document that belonged where Dan Schorr put—on the public record."

Harrison Salisbury, a former associate editor of *The New York Times* and the founder of its "op-ed" page, is another journalist I must mention here; for certainly he evidences flashes of the existential spirit. In an article in *The Columbia Journalism Review*,[34] Salisbury recounts how he ran into the conformist tendencies in the press (and the pressures from the White House and Pentagon) when he wrote a series of articles from Hanoi in late 1966 and early 1967. He also tells of correspondents in both the Korean and Vietnam wars who favored the imposition of censorship on their stories: "Apparently they thought censorship would remove the problem of confronting the moral issues of war reporting. Let the government decide what was right—or not right."[35] This, of course, would be a good example of Sartrean "bad faith"—a kind of escape from using freedom to make one's own choices and decisions.

Salisbury takes a definite existentialist position when he poses these questions about reporting: "Can we turn ourselves into computers? Should we try to divorce ourselves from the human race? Should we turn our backs on injustice? Why protect an objectivity which we do not and cannot possess? Would we all not be more honest—would not the reader be better served—if we carefully stated our prejudices and then did our best to tell the facts as we had discovered them to be?[36] *These are all important existential questions*! They, at least in large part, mark out some of the basic concerns of the existentialist in journalism. One's reaction to them, his attitude toward them, and his answers to them will serve to indicate whether or not he is existential or not in his basic journalistic stance.

A Few Concluding Remarks

Existential journalism begins with a kind of pessimism. Why? Because of a concern with death among existentialists generally, but in the case of journalism it is not so much the individual's

---

[34] *The Columbia Journalism Review* (Jan./Feb., 1976).

[35] *Ibid.*, p. 51.

[36] *Ibid.*, p. 53.

EXISTENTIAL JOURNALISM

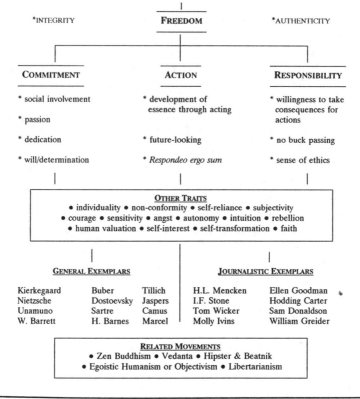

*INTEGRITY **FREEDOM** *AUTHENTICITY

COMMITMENT	**ACTION**	**RESPONSIBILITY**
* social involvement	* development of essence through acting	* willingness to take consequences for actions
* passion		
* dedication	* future-looking	* no buck passing
* will/determination	* *Respondeo ergo sum*	* sense of ethics

OTHER TRAITS
• individuality • non-conformity • self-reliance • subjectivity • courage • sensitivity • angst • autonomy • intuition • rebellion • human valuation • self-interest • self-transformation • faith

GENERAL EXEMPLARS			**JOURNALISTIC EXEMPLARS**	
Kierkegaard	Buber	Tillich	H.L. Mencken	Ellen Goodman
Nietzsche	Dostoevsky	Jaspers	I.F. Stone	Hodding Carter
Unamuno	Sartre	Camus	Tom Wicker	Sam Donaldson
W. Barrett	H. Barnes	Marcel	Molly Ivins	William Greider

RELATED MOVEMENTS
• Zen Buddhism • Vedanta • Hipster & Beatnik • Egoistic Humanism or Objectivism • Libertarianism

death, but the knowledge that press freedom is dying everywhere. It is disappearing rapidly. The journalism of the world is going toward authoritarianism everywhere. It is really the old process of entropy at work: the inclination of a system to run down, become passive. With such a recognition, the freedom-loving existential journalist naturally is anxious, develops a kind of *Angst*; but this anxiety does not debilitate the journalist—on the contrary, this very sense of the impending doom of journalistic freedom instills in him the desire to live fully his freedom while time remains.

The existential journalist has the conviction of the death of journalistic freedom; therefore, he must live every minute of every day in such a way as to maximize his own freedom and autonomy. He can thus create small "islands of decreasing entropy," as Norbert Wiener has put it.

This "sense of freedom's doom," this anxiety, leads to a concern for involvement, to a commitment to commitment. No more is the journalist satisfied to simply muddle through the day, doing the same old mechanistic duties, being caught in the ever-deepening rut in the newsroom. There is a new dedication to commitment, to making every day count, to pushing back the limits of restrictions, to suggesting the unorthodox, to daring to be honest—in short, to making oneself into an ever more authentic journalist and person.

Journalism is a way of life, and the journalist *exists* in this way. Acting journalistically is the main thing; having a theory about journalism is another, and of much lesser import. A code of ethics hanging on the wall is meaningless; a code of ethics internalized within the journalist and guiding his actions is what is meaningful. Action, really, and not theory is the thing that counts with the existentialist. Theory without action is dead. If all the "theory" and words about commitment and action which one hears at many journalism conventions were translated into action, there would truly be a revolution in the press. The freedom-loving, active, imaginative, and committed journalist is hard to find.

But, I can hear myriads of cautious organization-persons crying: Is there not a danger that existential journalists would pose problems for the viability and stability of the newspapers and other media? Wouldn't existential journalists go too far with this individualistic, creative urge? Wouldn't they go overboard and hurt the collective, corporate effort we're making?

My answer: Some of them well might. And, in many cases, it would be good if they did. We need a lot of fresh air blowing into most journalistic media. But, actually, there is nothing for the media managers and the conformist journalists to fear, for there is no serious danger from these existential journalists. They will simply not be numerous enough to pose any real danger to the ever-growing corporate structure of journalism.

I hope that this chapter has presented at least the main outlines of existential journalism in such a way that some clarification of the term has been made. Probably there are still many questions in the reader's mind as to just what existential journalism is. But at least a start has been made to explicate this journalistic orientation, and it is hoped that the chapters which follow will shed further light on the essential nature of existential journalism.

4

Pessimism, Anxiety, and Freedom

The Existentialist thinker feels solitary in the midst of today's society, cut off from nature, and the rest of humanity, his most intimate friends, and even his deepest self. This many-sided alienation weighs on him like an eternal fate that cannot be changed or conquered, even though man is obliged to contest against it.

—GEORGE NOVACK, *Existentialism versus Marxism*

Many young people, it is true, do not seem to value freedom. But some of us still believe that, without freedom, human beings cannot become fully human and that freedom is therefore supremely valuable. Perhaps the forces that now menace freedom are too strong to be resisted for very long. It is still our duty to do whatever we can to resist them.

—ALDOUS HUXLEY, *Brave New World Revisited*

TODAY'S JOURNALISTS, along with the rest of us, are caught up in something close to what the sociologists call *anomie*, the mechanistic and non-creative work that comprises our daily routine, a lack of fulfillment and isolation from a finished product, and the absence from participation in decision. This, the sociologists say, is at the root of a broad spiritual malaise; and this *anomie* certainly resembles the existentialists' concept of "alienation." It is the very *anomie*, say many sociologists, that works toward socialization, that leads persons to organize, to join, to lose themselves in a group or collectivity. This helps to wipe out the terrible feeling of alienation and personal anxiety. So, from one perspective, we can look on this feeling of alienation as a stimulus to socialization and a road to psychological comfort. Conforming and cooperating is, in a sense, a means of living harmoniously, not only with others but also with oneself.

This, however, is not the view of the existentialist. A person should *not* escape from the anxieties of life; he should not try to find safe havens of psychological conformity into which to flee from the violent storms of life. In fact, he should accept these buffetings, these feelings of alienation and anxiety as natural and necessary aspects of *true being*. The existentialist looks on this ontological anxiety as the catalyst to real *intensive* living. The journalist, for example, who escapes the vicissitudes of life through routinized and conformist journalism is, from an existentialist perspective, dead. He is "comfortable," perhaps, but his is the "comfort" of a stone or a tree. It is through striving, fighting, involving himself, suffering, and agonizing fully in the mainstream of life that he truly lives.

For the existentialist, the world is a rough and dangerous place; it is not to be fled and hidden from. It is to be faced squarely. The existentialist knows that dangers are all around him; it is this very recognition that causes him anxieties and anguish. He also knows that facing these dangers and living totally with the resulting anguish is what makes him truly a person and thrusts him into new and intensive levels of existence. He is not, like the utilitarian, seeking happiness; rather he is seeking total, true, *intensive* living.

Alienation in the Modern World

The journalist, at once isolated from society in his role as its reporter-interpreter and at the same time knowledgeable about the happenings of society, feels himself alienated. He lives in his own little verbal world of symbols abstracted from reality; he sees the world as scribbles on a page, images on a tube, or sounds from a speaker. He, in effect, tends to become a piece of transmitting machinery himself; he finds it difficult to retain his own personhood, his own identity, his own individuality as he routinely collects, packages, and transmits "the world" to others.

He almost becomes someone other than himself. Actually, as Jacques Ellul has pointed out, alienation largely means this very process: being someone other (*alienus*) than oneself. And, says Ellul, it also can mean to "belong to someone else," "to be deprived of one's self," "to be subjected to, or even identified with, someone else."[1] As the journalist *fits in* more and more snugly with his communication medium, he increasingly becomes "someone other" than himself; he belongs to *someone else* as he takes orders and ceases to exercise his own creativity. He is deprived of himself, detached from society (although he "reports" it), and lives in his own little world of corporate journalism in a passive, second-hand world created by himself and his colleagues.

Journalists, in their mainly neutralist, dispassionate role, become overly detached from society. They do, of course, come in contact with representatives of society, but mainly these persons are looked upon simply as "sources," as "participants," as "spokesmen"—in short, as *news*. According to Camus and other existentialists, this isolation of persons and groups from real life and vital society is growing; more and more, people in society are voluntarily and involuntarily being alienated. Perhaps Camus's novel *The Stranger* illustrates this isolation or estrangement as well as any literary work; it combines the issues of alienation, self-estrangement, the mechanization of the person and the general loss of true personhood.[2]

Robert Olson believes that, for the existentialist, the chief value in life is intensity—exemplified in acts of free choice, individual self-assertion, personal love, and creative work. And, says Olson, these various "forms of intensely lived experience are impossible without anguish, suffering, and risk."[3] One main cause of this suffering is what Olson calls the "anguish before the necessity of choosing"—what is often referred to as the "anguish of freedom." Erich Fromm deals with this in his *Escape from Freedom*, in which he observes that a man's loneliness is usually caused by freedom, and that when he achieves freedom, he tends to experience isolation, loneliness and even self-estrangement. So, with the existentialists, Fromm would say that a recognition (and use) of freedom is what brings about this alienation. In a later book, *The Revolution of Hope*, Fromm deals with ways

---

[1] Jacques Ellul, *Propaganda* (New York: Knopf—Vintage Books, 1973), p. 169.

[2] *The Stranger* (New York: Vintage Books, 1946).

[3] Robert G. Olson, *An Introduction to Existentialism* (New York: Dover Publications, Inc., 1962), p. 19.

technocracies aid in producing self-alienation and mechanization of action in human beings; he ties this trend to the decline of faith and the rise of scientism—the search for scientific truth. Modern man, according to Fromm, has concentrated on technical and material values and has lost the capacity for deep emotional experiences. The machines he has built, posits Fromm, have become so powerful that they have dehumanized him.[4]

Gabriel Marcel, the French Christian existentialist, also believes that technocracy—as well as large organizations—leads to this personal alienation of which Fromm speaks.[5] This impact of technology and organization will be taken up later in this chapter. Carl Jung places much of the blame for the estrangement—or as he puts it, "psychic isolation"—of the individual on the doorstep of the mass State. According to Jung, the State wants the person to be isolated, for "the more unrelated individuals are, the more consolidated the State becomes, and vice versa."[6]

Whatever the reasons for this alienation or estrangement, it is seen by existentialists as part of authentic living. It must be faced, and transcended by action; it must be overcome by an increased respect for Self. For, in effect, the existentialist considers alienation in chiefly inward terms; it is a person's alienation from his deepest being. As John Macquarrie says, an alienated person "is not himself but simply a cipher in the mass-existence of the crowd or a cog in the industrial system or whatever it may be."[7] The existentialist faces this alienation and turns it into a part of his true existence—a catalyst for intensive life. But we can see that mass society itself alienates—not only in separating persons from authentic relationships with others, but in separating them from their own true existence. Kierkegaard has stressed that man must function as an individual, but in meaningful relationship to other individuals, in order to overcome the corroding effects of alienation. He envisioned social man absorbed in a group or a crowd as "inhuman."[8]

---

[4] *The Revolution of Hope* (New York: Harper & Row, 1968), p. 2 ff.

[5] *Man Against Mass Society* (Chicago: Henry Regnery Co.—a Gateway Edition, 1969), p. 204.

[6] C. G. Jung, *The Undiscovered Self* (New York: Mentor Books, 1958), p. 115.

[7] *Existentialism* (New York: Penguin Books, 1973), p. 160.

[8] Nicholas A. Horvath, *Philosophy* (Woodbury, N.Y.: Barron's Educational Series Inc., 1974), p. 106.

Journalistic Anxiety and Anguish

Out of a background of alienation, anxiety and anguish—all really blending together like a black cloud over man—comes this pervading sense of pessimism that seems to mark all existentialists. Frustration, insecurity, and painful striving are the inescapable lot of mankind; however, some persons try to minimize this, try to escape from it, but the existentialist, as Robert Olson has said, looks on this dismal situation as something to be squarely faced: it is only in so confronting the pain and dangers of life that life is worth living. Olson adds that a life of frustration, insecurity, and anguish produces values, and "the values so generated are the only ones actually realizable and genuinely worthy of human pursuit."[9]

Meeting life squarely, loving the struggle, and avoiding any temptation to seek safety in seclusion: this is a main message of the existentialist. This refrain, with many variations, has been heard many times through the years. Listen to the words of Henry David Thoreau:

> However mean your life is, meet it and live; do not shun it and call it hard names. It is not so bad as you are. It looks poorest when you are richest. The fault-finder will find faults even in paradise. Love your life, poor as it is.[10]

What is this "anxiety" (or *Angst*) that encompasses the person? It is difficult to explain, for it is a feeling, a sense, a kind of dismal premonition. The existentialists seem to have in mind a subtle emotion of "uneasiness" or "malaise"; sometimes they use the terms "dread" and "anguish," but usually "anxiety" appears to be the best English word to describe it. Anxiety is linked to freedom, often described as the "vertigo" or "dizziness" of freedom.[11]

> Anxiety arises rather because "I distrust myself and my own reactions" (Sartre). In other words, there is a profound ambiguity in freedom—hence the paradoxical expression we are *condemned* to be free. A nothingness slips into my action. I am not the self that I will be, or I am it in the mode of not being it.[12]

---

[9] Olson, p. 14.

[10] *Thoreau on Man and Nature*, a compilation of writings of Thoreau by A. D. Volkman (Mt. Vernon, N.Y.: The Peter Pauper Press, 1960), p. 24.

[11] Macquarrie, p. 129.

[12] *Ibid*., p. 131.

This idea of not being what I will be, this idea of "nothing-ness" at the moment, is important to the existentialist, and, as Macquarrie points out above, is responsible for much of the anxiety which we have. The journalist is suspended, as it were, between two moments of nothingness; he senses that he is constantly headed toward the annihilation of his own contingency—*In der Welt zum Tode sein*, as Heidegger puts it. Frederick Patka interprets this in the following short passage:

> I am what I was, that is, nothing; I also am what I will be, that is, nothing again, for past and future as such are located outside the horizon of actuality. This experience of anguish and dread, conditioned by the awareness of one's complete contingency, is of the greatest value to the existentialists, for they believe that it is here at this crucial moment of personal crisis that the "opening for transcendence" emerges.[13]

Anxiety does not only arise from our recognition of freedom or from the sense of our constant hanging between two points of "nothingness"; it also tends to well up from within us as an "uncanny apprehension of some impending evil, of something not within us, but of an alien power."[14] And, for some, anxiety is seen as "despair" and despair is "the sickness unto death."[15] One type of anxiety is caused by "self-estrangement"—not external, but something going on in the person himself. Kier-kegaard heralded the Age of Anxiety; it is now full upon us.

Jacques Ellul says that anxiety (which he equates with psychological fear) is perhaps "the most widespread psychologi-cal trait in our society." Of course, says Ellul, we have good reasons to be afraid—"of Communist subversion, revolution, Fascism, H-bombs, conflict between East and West, unemploy-ment, sickness." He points out that on one hand the number of dangers is increasing, and the news media make us more aware of them, and on the other hand, religious beliefs, which allowed man to face fear, have almost disappeared. "Man is disarmed," Ellul says, "in the face of the perils threatening him, and is increasingly alarmed by these perils because he keeps reading about them."[16] Consciousness of all these dangers, coupled with

---

[13] *Existentialist Thinkers and Thought* (New York: The Citadel Press, 1966), p. 66.

[14] F. H. Heinemann, *Existentialism and the Modern Predicament* (New York: Harper Torchbooks, 1958), p. 36.

[15] *Ibid.*, p. 37.

[16] Ellul, p. 153.

the concept of self-estrangement, brings on this anxiety; the person becomes bewildered and frightened, and, as George Novack says, "such bewildered and frightened individuals can not help questioning their most trustworthy values and cherished creeds."[17]

For many people, anxiety is brought on—or heightened—by a sense of loss of personhood, a sense of insignificance in the face of increasing State and social control. Such State encroachment on the individual, of course, has not just begun, but it is gaining momentum. Here is Roderick Seidenberg, talking about the conflict in the modern world between the State and the individual:

> ... it is interesting to note, during the nineteenth century virtu-ally every free and noble-spirited writer from Tolstoy to Thoreau, from Kropotkin to Emerson, rose in defense of the Great Tradition and the integrity of the individual against the steady encroach-ments of the state. But today it is no longer the state alone that is in conflict with the implications of these doctrines: it is a wider system of things wherein the state itself, in its supreme and sovereign aspects, is being drawn into the orbit of largr, world-wide agglomerations. Nor will the totalitarian pattern that has crept from the state fail to emerge in these larger spheres of international scope. ... As the gravitational force of the mass increases, that of the individual decreases, relatively as well as actually, until a final condition of solidarity and conformity is attained.[18]

Seidenberg sees in the future an "ultimate stabilization of human relationships" and an "abatement and exclusion of all change and variation"; thus, at length, predicts Seidenberg, man will find himself "in an ever more securely established milieu—in a period of unchanging continuity."[19] For some, these may be comforting words—but for the existentialist who prizes freedom, change, and the combative spirit, they are anything but comfort-ing. But, while they are not comforting to the existentialist, they are not debilitating—in fact, they simply describe a state that must be faced and transcended.

---

[17] George Novack (ed.), *Existentialism versus Marxism* (New York: Dell Publishing Co.—Delta Books, 1966), p. 7.

[18] Roderick Seidenberg, *Posthistoric Man: An Inquiry* (New York: The Viking Press, 1974), pp. 230-31.

[19] *Ibid.*, p. 237.

Social and Journalistic Causes for Pessimism

The individual looks around him and sees a multitude of problems. He has good reason to be pessimistic. He has good reason to be anxious. He even has good reason to be forlorn and dismal in his outlook. Corruption is to be found on all sides; crime is increasing; population is getting out of hand; the world seems to be fast losing its capacity for hope; pornography is proliferating; brainpower is being mobilized for destructive purposes; personal safety is being increasingly endangered; millions are living a marginal existence on the brink of starvation; a sense of morality is almost totally absent in business and politics; educational standards are crumbling; illiteracy is growing—and there are innumerable other signs portending a dismal future.

The situation in journalism itself is equally dismal. Freedom in journalism is disappearing everywhere; a "sameness" is spreading throughout the press as journalistic monopolies and conglomerates increase; advertising is fast encasing journalism in a slick, emotional, irrational, and propagandistic patina, corrosive to cultured thought and language; journalism education— ever more "professional" in the sense of becoming standardized—is pouring out increasing numbers of poorly educated, mechanistic robots who find it difficult to write a correct sentence; and the public itself—and not only the government—is becoming suspicious of the press, finding it careless, inaccurate, unbelievable, and generally unreliable. Any person who has first-hand knowledge of an event and sees a report of it in the press knows very well how superficial, distorted, and inaccurate modern journalism is. Journalism is, indeed, increasingly under fire. And there are few indications that it is heading toward better days.

H. L. Mencken would have plenty of support today for his words about the press, written in 1920: "What ails the newspapers of the United States primarily . . . is the fact that their gigantic commercial development compels them to appeal to larger and larger masses of undifferentiated men, and that the truth is a commodity that the masses of undifferentiated men cannot be induced to buy."[20] And these biting words of Mencken still produce nods of approval today:

---

[20] H. L. Mencken, *A Gang of Pecksniffs*, ed. by Theo Lippman, Jr. (New Rochelle, N.Y.: Arlington House, 1975), p. 64.

The *average* American newspaper, *especially* of the so-called better sort, has the intelligence of a Baptist evangelist, the courage of a rat, the fairness of a Prohibitionist boob-bumper, the information of a high-school janitor, the taste of a designer of celluloid valentines, and the honor of a police-station lawyer.[21]

Mencken saw the newspapers (and they are still seen by many today) as being in the business of "snouting out and exhibiting new and startling horrors, atrocities, impending calamities, tyrannies, villainies, enormities, mortal perils, jeopardies, outrages, catastrophies—first snouting out and exhibiting them, and then magnificently circumventing and disposing of them."[22] Perhaps Mencken's harshest indictments of the American newspaper are found in this passage:

It is a mass of trivialities and puerilities; to recite it would be to make even a barber beg for mercy. What is missing from it, in brief, is everything worth knowing—everything that enters into the common knowledge of educated man. There are managing editors in the United States, and scores of them, who have never heard of Kant or Johannes Muller and never read the Constitution of the United States; there are city editors who do not know what a symphony is, or a streptococcus, or the Statute of Frauds; there are reporters by the thousands who could not pass the entrance examination for Harvard or Tuskegee, or even Yale. It is this vast and militant ignorance, this widespread and fathomless prejudice against intelligence, that makes American journalism so pathetically feeble and vulgar, and so generally disreputable.[23]

More recently (in 1971) Herbert I. Schiller has noted that "the information process in the United States continues to rest firmly in the grip of tenacious stand-patters." He further opines that these "stand-patters" are simply not capable of doing the job of explaining to their audiences the changes which are appearing in society—at home and abroad.[24] Schiller blasts the American press for being propagandistic, imperialistic, anti-progressive, etc., in this extremely critical appraisal of U.S. journalism.

Even Edward J. Epstein, a press critic whose comments on the press are generally considered moderate, has said that it is

---

[21] *Ibid.*, p. 63.
[22] *Ibid.*, p. 65.
[23] *Ibid.*, p. 130-131.
[24] Herbert I. Schiller, *Mass Communications and American Empire* (Boston: Beacon Press, 1971), p. 154.

practically impossible for Americans to get the truth from the press. He notes that Walter Lippmann also had concluded pessimistically "that if the public required a more truthful interpretation of the world they lived in, they would have to depend on institutions other than the press."[25] Epstein adds that journalists cannot claim authority (such as that granted to academic researchers) because they cannot fulfill the requirements of always identifying their sources, and he says that "without identifiable sources the account cannot be reviewed or corroborated by others with specialized knowledge of the subject," and that therefore "even the most egregious errors may thus remain uncorrected."[26]

Ben Bagdikian, another contemporary press critic, writing of the large American daily newspapers, says that "a few are excellent, more are mediocre, and many are wretched."[27] And, as to the small dailies and weeklies in America, Bagdikian believes they are "the backyard of the trade, repositories for any piece of journalistic junk tossed over the fence, run as often by the printshop proprietors as by editors."[28] And, Jack Anderson, a reporter who evidences many existentialist traits, raps the press for not doing enough investigative reporting and for being too timid and passive. "Investigative reporters," he says, "must work harder, dig deeper, and verify their facts more carefully than establishment reporters."[29]

I, myself, could add many other negative observations about the press which would bespeak of the pessimistic outlook which can be taken by the journalist (or any other person) as he looks about the journalistic landscape. However, I shall refrain from doing this at present, and simply say that the basic "corporate" nature of the mass media and the increasing conformity and depersonalization found in all parts of our journalism is what I see as the most pessimistic indicator for the future. And from this conformist tendency emerges the dismal conclusion (at least for all libertarians and existentialists): that press freedom generally,

[25] Edward J. Epstein, *Between Fact and Fiction: The Problem of Journalism* (New York: Random House—Vintage Books, 1975), p. 4.

[26] *Ibid.*, p. 8.

[27] Ben Bagdikian, *The Effete Conspiracy and Other Crimes by the Press* (New York: Harper & Row—Colophon Books, 1974), p. 8.

[28] *Ibid.*, p. 47.

[29] Jack Anderson, *The Anderson Papers* (New York: Random House—Ballantine Books, 1974), p. 9.

and personal journalistic autonomy specifically, is lying on the sickbed throughout the world at the very door of death.

The Specter of Technology and Organization

One of the chief dangers to press freedom (and to freedom generally) is the impact of technology and organization on the individual life of a person. The journalist finds that he has less and less incentive, encouragement, or chance to exert his own creativity; he knows that his organization demands more and more of his time and effort. He conforms or he suffers. So generally he conforms. What else can he do? This is the normal question which he asks; and this question presents his rationalization for submitting himself to the encroachment of technology and organization.

He can, of course, rebel. He can meet the life-facts and life-forces head-on. He can agitate. He can individualize himself through *his attitude* toward technology and organization. He can know that this attitude forces him to fight constantly to retain as much self-determinism and self-respect as possible. Certainly, he can not escape the benumbing influence of technology altogether; but he can fling himself enthusiastically into the fight for self-preservation. He can glory in the *tension* of the struggle. For he knows that when the struggle stops—and he capitulates to the machine and the organization—*as a person* he is dead.

And, of course, he can always change jobs. He can quit if the restrictions become so strict that he is unable even to struggle against them. But this is not the existential journalist's way: he prefers to remain in the fray—not in order to change the organization to *his* type of organization, for he is against *all* organizations. He wants to stay in the struggle for the simple reason that the intensity and constant tension is where real life is. In spite of this proclivity to struggle, the existential journalist recognizes the fact that growing technology and organization are forces which level society and make it more difficult for the person to direct his own life. In this sense he can look on organization (and its accompanying technology) as degrading to the person, as tragic barriers to self-fulfillment, and as potent contributors to a pessimistic outlook.

Organizations exert a great pull on the individual. In journalism this is especially true; for not only the complexity of the news institution itself, with its proliferating hierarchy, but the expanding reliance on computers and other machines that increasingly take decisions out of the hands of the individual journalist. Michael Novak bemoans this growing embrace of scientism in these words:

> The more science and technology advance, the clearer their inner dynamic becomes. They are not directed toward the good of concrete, individual human beings but toward efficiency. The primary goal of scientific knowledge is power; the primary goal of technology is efficiency. Neither power nor efficiency has a necessary relation to the integrity of persons.[30]

The journalist is easily caught up in the organization. He is, as H. L. Mencken has noted, "forced to make himself an instrument of enterprises that he sometimes cannot understand and must often regard as sinister." How does this affect him? Mencken adds that the journalist "ends by losing all sense of public responsibility, and so becomes a mere kept blackguard, ready at the word of command to defend the guilty or to harass and persecute the innocent."[31] The journalist is prone to become "an instrument," as Mencken calls him, because of the temptation to lose himself in the organization; in a real sense the average journalist wants to conform, to operate in highly predictable and harmonious ways. What Lewis Yablonsky calls "robopathic patterns" are insidious; they are prone to dominate rather quickly any newspaper or other journalistic medium. They creep in, spread, and subtly dehumanize the editorial staff until it becomes nothing more than a corporate mill, grinding out its routine and bland products in ever more impersonal ways.[32]

Unfortunately, it is very difficult (all but impossible) for the journalist to work independently; he is forced by the nature of

---

[30] Michael Novak, *The Experience of Nothingness* (New York: Harper Colophon Books, 1971), p. 34.

[31] Mencken, pp. 60-70.

[32] The routinized and highly structured world of pragmatic journalism affects the practitioner greatly, making him a good "organization" man, causing him to respect the hierarchy, to take orders docilely from his "superiors." The average journalist is shaped rather quickly into a good "team player," and this is why so often when these persons gravitate to the faculties of schools and departments of journalism, they have a difficult time understanding the academic life with its spirit of individualism. They miss the "order," the smooth-functioning of their old mass medium, and they are irritated and often stunned by the seeming chaos and independence of the "academic types."

journalism to be a part of an organization—to "join" a mass medium. This fact, at the outset, limits his individuality and diminishes his Self. And this very fact is what has caused some potentially good journalists, like Ernest Hemingway, to leave journalism for literature—or, at last to practice journalism only occasionally and peripherally.

In view of the basic nature of journalism, it is easy to see why the existentialist finds in journalism a difficult and unsympathetic home. He enters journalism normally by sublimating his individuality to the organization; he forfeits his creativity to the "system"; he permits the editors to change—and often mutilate—his copy; he passes his day writing what he is told to write, doing what he is told to do; he has little incentive or energy to "do his own thing."

If the average journalist stopped to think about it, he would realize that he, like Camus' Sisyphus, is constantly rolling the heavy stone of news and opinion up the hill of daily journalism only to have it slide back down the slippery slope; he goes on with this routine rolling throughout his journalistic life, repetitiously repeating his tasks—doing the same old journalistic tasks in the same old ways—day after day after day. Most journalists, however, *do not stop to think about it.* They are oblivious to this meaninglessness of their journalism. But the existential journalist does think about it, and this consciousness of the basic absurdity of it all is what gives his activity meaning. Michael Novak puts it this way:

> I perceive the ambiguity of my own conscious life. I recognize the formlessness, the aimlessness, and the disunity implicit in my own insignificance, my mortality, my ultimate dissolution. I peer into madness, chaos, and death. These insights are true insights. Not to experience them is to evade the character of one's own consciousness. It is to live a lie. The experience of nothingness bears the taste of honesty.[33]

In order to try to escape the aimlessness, the pain and anxiety of the existential situation, most journalists submit to the organization and lose themselves in the system. The organizing instinct is very powerful. Carl Jung notes the power of groupism and organization when he writes that "individual judgment grows increasingly uncertain of itself and . . . responsibility is collec-

---

[33] Novak, p. 15.

tivized as much as possible, i.e., is shuffled off by the individual and delegated to a corporate body."[34] Jung also notes that "people go on blithely organizing and believing in the sovereign remedy of mass action,"[35] but that "ultimately everything depends on the quality of the individual." H. L. Mencken blasts journalism for having too many practictioners who "are still slaves and they look and act the part," who belong to press clubs and who take a "childish pride in a puerile Philistinism, and are still far too willing to do anything they are ordered to do, absolutely without challenge."[36]

Fewer and fewer individuals appear capable of standing out from the conformist organizational types. Seidenberg, in his *Posthistoric Man*, writes:

> The dominance of the collective aspects of man is inherently assured; and with it the gradual conversion of the individual into a frictionless and depersonalized member of the community. For the individual as such will be absorbed in the shadow of his collectivized self.[37]

The conditions of modern life do, undoubtedly, arouse in the individual a sense of futility and personal insignificance. It is to this feeling of one's worthlessness that Kierkegaard attributes the urge to organize—to combine with others. Kierkegaard, one of the foremost opponents of this Hegelian emphasis on "objectivity," calls the "uncritical desire to join the group a form of mass hysteria, and traces it to a wish to be stimulated by others and to be drawn out of one's own emptiness into at least a quantitative fullness and stability."[38]

Charles Frankel adds his voice to those who believe that technology—in addition to organization—tends to enslave us. Technological innovations, he says, are often introduced "without established mechanisms for appraising or controlling or even cushioning their consequences." The engineers who introduce them, according to Frankel, make decisions which have enormous power to affect the quality and conditions of our lives; "if they came dressed as social planners many of us would regard

---

[34] Jung, *The Undiscovered Self*, p. 26.
[35] *Ibid.*, p. 68.
[36] Mencken, *A Gang of Pecksniffs*, p. 85.
[37] Seidenberg, pp. 112-13.
[38] James Collins, *The Mind of Kierkegaard* (Chicago: Henry Regnery Co.— Gateway Edition, 1967), p. 192.

them as tyrants," he adds.[39] Gabriel Marcel has been particularly critical of what he has called "technocracy"—the all-prevading power of technology and its nilhilistic misuse in society. Marcel fears that in a technocracy "men may become *submen*, more and more reduced to their own specialized function within the. . . machine."[40]

Never have so many seemingly "normal" persons in our society been so "sick," according to Aldous Huxley. These persons are "normal," says Huxley, "not in what may be called the absolute sense of the word; they are normal only in relation to a profoundly abnormal society." And, Huxley adds, their "perfect adjustment to that abnormal society is a measure of their mental sickness."[41] Quoting Erich Fromm, Huxley notes that these millions of "abnormally normal people" are well-adjusted, but if they were "fully human beings" they would not be adjusted. And, Huxley continues, the conformity in society is developing into something like uniformity—and "uniformity and freedom are incompatible."[42]

So, I think it logical to conclude from the swirl of quotations given above, that one theme emerges: organization and technology are making the majority of persons conformists, are depersonalizing them, and making them tame and timid "robopaths." The existentialist, of course, fights against this tendency. He would certainly agree with these words of Thoreau:

> Undoubtedly, all men are not equally fit subjects for civilization; and because the majority, like dogs and sheep, are tame by inherited disposition, this is no reason why the others should have their natures broken that they may be reduced to the same level.[43]

The Cyclic-Entropic Hypothesis

One of the main causes for pessimism among existential journalists is the belief that press freedom is dying throughout

[39] Charles Frankel, *The Case for Modern Man* (Boston: Beacon Press, 1971), p. 198.

[40] Heinemann, p. 153.

[41] Huxley, p. 21.

[42] *Ibid.*, pp. 21-22.

[43] From Thoreau's essay "Walking" in Carl Bode (ed.), *The Portable Thoreau* (New York: The Viking Press, 1947), p. 619.

the world. This is much like the basic existentialist awareness of individual death, and the *angst* or anxiety which the facing of this fact brings. In the context of journalism, the existentialist knows that he must face the "death of freedom"—and he is determined to make use of this freedom while it lasts. Or, at least, he is convinced that he must exercise to the maximum the freedom which remains; he is *existential,* rather than theoretical, in his relationship to freedom. In other words, he is different from many "libertarians" in that he *lives* his freedom, rather than simply theorizing about it, or urging it in philosophical discourse. The existentialist is *always* a libertarian, but the libertarian is not always an existentialist; for the libertarian may be a "theoretical" libertarian, but the existentialist *cannot* be a "theoretical" existentialist since his existentialism must be *lived.*

Many thinkers have contributed to the pessimism stemming from the belief that freedom is dying and that all of society—not just the press—is gravitating toward a time of authoritarianism, passivity, and conformity. Many versions, timetables, etc. have been proposed for this trend toward an authoritarian society, but in every one on the net result is the same: a nondynamic, passive, totalitarian society which discourages individualism and freedom and encourages stability, harmony, and Statist and organizational paternalism.

Karl Mannheim talks of an historical cycle reminiscent of Nietzsche and Comte; he distinguishes three stages of development—the medieval man in collective solidarity, the post-Renaissance man in individual competition, and the presently emerging man steeped in "group solidarity." It is this third category toward which we are presenting drifting—and it applies equally to man in Communist, Fascist, and liberal-capitalist cultures, for the factor which Mannheim sees as uniting them all "is the phenomenon of Great Society which the industrial revolution has brought into being."[44] The pull of organizations, discussed in the previous section, largely accounts for this drift toward conformity and authoritarianism, for, as Carl Jung says, "people go on blithely organizing and believing in the sovereign remedy of mass action, without the least consciousness of the fact that the most powerful organizations can be main-

---

[44] Brian V. Hill, *Education and the Endangered Individual* (New York: Dell Publishing Co., 1973), p. 111.

tained only by the greatest ruthlessness of their leaders and the cheapest of slogans."[45]

Roderick Seidenberg insists that the principle of organization leads to "the ultimate state of crystallization" in a society, which results in "patterns of frigid and unalterable perfection."[46] Man will accept this fate, according to Seidenberg, for he will feel that this "centripetal pull of organization as a kind of social gravitation, at once universal, inescapable, and beneficient." Seidenberg also believes that the principle of organization breeds more organization—the idea of "One World" illustrates this trend, says Seidenberg, and "it has been in process from the beginning."[47] Carl Jung notes that the individual becomes more and more a function of society; in reality, he says, the State "drifts into the situation of a primitive form of society, namely the communism of a primitive tribe where everybody is subject to the autocratic rule of a chief or an oligarchy."[48]

Seidenberg postulates that the present century is the Century of Transition: an interim period from historic age to posthistoric age, a final age of historic slowing down, conformity, loss of energy, smooth-running organization, and passivity.[49] He points out that there is no real reason to believe in limitless progress and development for a society:

> The readily accepted notion that history will inevitably follow a continuous course without break or climax, devoid of any possible comprehensive transformations, and basic and significant changes of phase, must be held to be as arbitrary, dogmatic, and essentially unimaginative as the contrary notion that history is a directionless chaos.[50]

This picture is, indeed, a gloomy one. Or at least it is a gloomy one to the existentialist who frets in social stagnation, however placid such a society might be. He hates to think of this future drift from "the organic to the inorganic, from the living to the mechanical," as Seidenberg has put it.[51] He, like Seidenberg,

---

[45] C. G. Jung, p. 68.

[46] Seidenberg, p. 180.

[47] *Ibid.*, p. 134.

[48] Jung, pp. 26-27.

[49] Seidenberg, p. 85. Cf., J. B. Bury, *The Idea of Progress* (New York: Macmillan, 1932).

[50] Seidenberg, p. 67.

[51] *Ibid.*

sees in this trend "the lineaments of a Spenglerian doom not only of our Western culture along with that of the world at large but, as we have seen, of the individual *per se* as well."[52]

*   *   *

This brings me back again to journalistic pessimism, a pessimism based on this drift toward authoritarianism and on the recognition that press freedom has a terminal illness. On the basis of this belief, reinforced by a whole array of writers (who may not have put it so bluntly), I would like to present a hypothesis which I am calling the Cyclic-Entropic Hypothesis of Journalistic Freedom and Development. Here it is:

> A media system or a single medium develops slowly in its initial stages during a rather static, non-energetic and conformist period, gathering momentum for a time during a more energetic and pluralistic period, and then flattening out into a more bland, less energetic, more conservative state where stability and lack of friction, coupled with a gravitational pull toward collectivistic conformity, sends the medium or system into an extended period of passivity or into the oblivion of death.

The concept of *entropy* is worked into this hypothesis for it is felt that it is quite consistent with a cyclic theory of social systems. Entropy is derived from the Second Law of Thermodynamics, which says in effect that all systems tend to run down, dissolve, lose energy. This tendency to "run down" (entropy) has been a theme applied not only by physicists and engineers, but also by social scientists and historians (e.g., Henry Adams) dating from the first part of this century.

Since journalism can be looked on as a system (also, its parts as systems), there seems no reason why the concept of entropy cannot be applied to it. So it is hypothesized here that media systems will lose energy, become passive, and conformist. Norbert Wiener, who has written much about entropy, notes this increasing conformity when he says that sooner or later there will be "nothing left but a drab uniformity out of which we can expect only minor and insignificant local fluctuations."[53] He talks about the whole universe dying "the heat death" where the world will

---

[52] *Ibid.*, p. 207.

[53] Norbert Wiener, *The Human Use of Human Beings: Cybernetics and Society* (New York: Avon Books—Discus Edition, 1967), p. 45.

be reduced to one vast temperature equilibrium, but the concept might also be applied to journalistic systems. Wiener presents, in the fact of this impending entropic disaster an extremely existentialist demeanor:

> In a very real sense we are shipwrecked passengers on a doomed planet. Yet even in a shipwreck, human decencies and human values do not necessarily vanish, and we must make the most of them. We shall go down, but let it be in a manner to which we may look forward as worthy of our dignity.[54]

Paraphrased for the journalistic context, this might be that journalists are employees of a doomed craft—at least so far as its vitality and freedom are concerned. Yet the dignity of the individual journalist and the basic value of freedom still exist, and we in journalism must make the most of them. The freedom-loving journalist will be defeated; he will meet frustration time and time again, but his struggle for freedom and authenticity should be such that it is worthy of his dignity.

There are many indications of the shrinking freedom of the press in the world; annual reports by the International Press Institute, the Inter American Press Association, the University of Missouri's Freedom of Information Center and other groups and organizations show a steady trend toward press control. This is all well summed up in John Tebbel's excellent little book, *Media in America* (1974), where a pessimistic picture is painted. Tebbel quotes Alexander Hamilton who said in 1788 that liberty of the press must altogether "depend on public opinion, and on the general spirit of the people and of the government." Tebbel offers this stark warning: "If the 'general spirit of the people and of the government' is the only guarantee of a free press today, its demise is assured unless that spirit changes in both the governed and their governors."[55] And Jerome Tuccille adds his words to the warning of Tebbel:

> If government continues its intrusion into the nation's broadcasting industry, it will unquestionably be only a matter of time before total control is attempted over the publishing business, the film industry, and virtually every other commercial channel of communications in the country. When this happens, when government has succeeded in destroying freedom of speech, free-

---

[54] *Ibid.*, p. 58.

[55] John Tebbel, *The Media in America* (New York: New American Library—Mentor Books, 1974), p. 431.

dom of expression—when it has, in effect, eliminated an effective *verbal opposition* to its own policies—we will then be witnessing the beginning of a genuine totalitarian regime and the final destruction of all pretense of liberty in the United States of America.[56]

Each existential journalist will, while recognizing the coming death of press freedom about which these writers warn, determine to slow its coming as much as possible through individual effort, to create what Wiener calls "islands of decreasing entropy." This, of course, will serve only to hold back the final demise of press freedom; it will grant more time, but there is no reason for the existential journalist to think he can reverse the trend. For the signs are clear all around us that there is a growing demand for "order" and "responsibility" in journalism, and entropy is associated with "order" and lack of friction—a kind of equilibrium and harmony resulting from passivity.[57]

This natural drift toward less friction, less energy, to a kind of running down of the human spirit has been seen as "inevitable" by many writers. Seidenberg, for example, calls this final passive stage of society or systems "post-historic"; it will be devoid of change, passive, conformist, endless routine—"not unlike that of the ants, the bees, and the termites."[58] This entropic tendency can be applied to social systems, and has been. In a volume by J. F. Klein (*The Physical Significance of Entropy*), a work based directly upon the interpretations of two outstanding authorities in the field of thermodynamics, Boltzmann and Planck, is found the following pertinent passage:

> The Second Law of Thermodynamics has no *independent* significance, for its roots go down deep into the Theory of Probability. It is therefore conceivable that it is applicable to some purely human and animate events as well as inanimate, natural events. . . .[59]

Freedom and individualism were enthroned in the Nineteenth Century in the journalism of the Western World. To

---

[56] Jerome Tucille, *Radical Libertarianism* (New York: Perennial Library, 1971), p. 107.

[57] Joseph Needham, *Time: The Refreshing River* (New York: Macmillan, 1943), p. 220.

[58] Seidenberg, p. 170.

[59] J. F. Klein, *The Physical Signifcance of Entropy* (New York: D. Van Nostrand Co., 1919), p. 90.

some degree, Western journalism is still so inclined; this has been the era of the individualist; it is, however, fast-disappearing and, as Seidenberg has said, "once past will never again return."[60] He sees the eclipse of the individual as implicit in all the trends pointing to the future. He states: "In the confusion of forces that confront us nothing is plainer than the steady drift toward ever wider and more inclusive social relationships and, by the same token, a corresponding pressure upon the individual toward great conformity, coherence, and compliance in ever wider arcs of life."[61]

In this final passive, conformist phase of entropy toward which we are headed, the creative individual will have all but disappeared; for when society "tends toward a condition of stability, security, and eventual sterility, the exceptional men are doomed *a fortiori* to impotence and extinction; for in that society either they will not arise or they will be suppressed."[62] Oswald Spengler sees this final entropic stage (his "Civilization" as contrasted to an earlier "Culture" stage) as a *scientific* stage characterized as "artificial, rootless," and mechanistic. It is obvious that the existentialist would find such a world not to his liking; for in Spengler's words this "scientific" world would be superficial, practical, and soulless, where life would be "no longer lived as something self-evident—hardly a matter of consciousness, let alone choice ... but presented as the intellect sees it, judged by 'utilitarian' or 'rational' criteria. . . ."[63]

Toynbee sees this ultimate stage as an imitative, non-creative stage, also. The mass of people lack challenges and creative energy. Speaking of civilizations, Toynbee says that once a civilization has broken down, it follows an inexorable and melancholy path. He points out that civilizations (and systems, too?) grow best when conditions are difficult so as to stir up a high degree of energy and *elan* in the people. When challenge is gone, he says, civilizations begin to decay; conformity sets in, and energy dissipates (entropy accelerates). It is then that society enters Toynbee's "Time of Troubles," which would roughly correspond to Spengler's late autumn or early winter stage.[64]

---

[60] Seidenberg, p. 86.

[61] *Ibid.*

[62] *Ibid.*, p. 218.

[63] Oswald Spengler, *The Decline of the West* (New York: Alfred A. Knopf, Inc., 1926), pp. 352-53.

[64] Charles Frankel, *The Case for Modern Man* (Boston: Beacon Press, 1971), pp. 174-75.

Seidenberg sees this posthistoric period as a period of "stability and permanence" symmetrical with, if not precisely equivalent to, that of man's earliest period.[65] He views history, then, as marked off with a transitional period—"a period of ever-increasing change, tending toward a climax, after which man may again attain, in perhaps an equally long interval of time, a relatively fixed state of stability and permanence."[66] This evidences a kind of historical drift from instinct to intelligence, exhibiting determinism, and evidencing cyclic characteristics. And it leads from the creative transitional period (which is presently ending) toward a non-creative, uniform, collectivist stage. Man thinks more; at the same time society gets more complex; there is more need for social direction or social engineering to retain social equilibrium; populations increase; chances for mass destruction increase. Therefore, man will use his increased intelligence to plan for stability, to direct mankind toward a happy, paternalistic, stable world. Also operative here is the existentialist notion—described psychologically so well by Erich Fromm—that man's basic nature is "to escape from freedom," or to live "in bad faith," as Sartre would put it.

Nikolai Berdyaev, also, thinks a cyclic social theory is valid, and rejects the concept of natural continuous progress of social systems. He sees the present century as a transitory period between a dying Humanist phase and an emerging "New Middle Ages"—a disciplining phase, a time of social fusion.[67] In this new "disciplining" or conformist period into which we are heading, Albert Schweitzer sees a decrease in creative thinking and an increase in superficial "mob-mindedness" formed by various "manufacturers of public opinion."[68] As he described it in his *Philosophy of Civilization* (1949), the main problem confronting us is the ethical, and he agrees with Spengler that the verbal concern and emphasis on the ethical indicates the last gasp of a dying civilization.

Walter Schubart feels, also, that we are standing before a new period of social stability, ushered in largely by a pervasive fear. He sees Promethean (individualistic) Culture dying and being

---

[65] Seidenberg, p. 56.

[66] *Ibid.*

[67] Pitirim A. Sorokin, *Modern Historical and Social Philosophies* (New York: Dover Publications, Inc., 1963), p. 139.

[68] *Ibid.*, p. 179.

replaced by an Oriental (collectivistic-cooperative) Culture.[69] Schubart, like these others mentioned, rejects the linear interpretation of history with its continuous progress. He postulates three main developmental stages for society: (1) the Harmonious, where man lives consonant with the world, (2) the Heroic, where man has domination over the world, and (3) the Ascetic, where man runs away (escapes) from the world.[70] This Ascetic stage is roughly equivalent to Berdyaev's "New Middle Ages," to Spengler's "Winter," to Toynbee's "Time of Troubles," to Schubart's "Oriental Culture," and to Seidenberg's "Posthistoric" Period.

*   *   *

Now, after giving some background for cyclic theories and for social system *entropy*, I should return to the hypothesis presented earlier in this section. The tendency of press systems to "run down" and the growing inclination to conform and to come to a static, harmonious state (after going through an "energetic" period) can be blended into a cyclic-entropic model of development. This is what I have done in the framing of this hypothesis, especially relating it to the growth and later demise of freedom in a press system. And, I see no reason why even the individual journalist cannot be seen as going through the same progression—from childish reliance, to youthful optimism, experimentalism and energy, to mature intelligent and cautious action, to old age timidity, passivity, paternalism, and loss of energy. This, of course, draws heavily on Spengler's four-stage typology.[71]

In framing this Cyclic-Entropic Journalistic Developmental Hypothesis, I have drawn on many sources,[72] but have relied mainly on those indicated in the brief chart which follows:

AUTHOR(S)	CHANGE: ROUGH STAGES		
Pye-Lerner-Schramm	Traditional	Transitional	Modern
Merrill	Authoritarian	Libertarian	Authoritarian

---

[69] Walter Schubart, *Europa und die Seele des Ostens* (Lucerne, 1938), pp. 313-18.

[70] *Ibid.*, pp. 13-16.

[71] Sorokin, pp. 90-93.

[72] The main works of these authors can be found in the bibliography.

Seidenberg	Prehistoric Historic Posthistoric
Berdyaev	Primitive Humanist New Middle Ages
Schubart	Harmonious Heroic Ascetic/Oriental
Sorokin	Sensate Ideational Eclectic
Spengler	Spring Summer Autumn Winter
Huxley/Orwell	Tribalism Individualism Collectivism
Wiener/Klein	energy increase max. energy energy decrease
Ellul	"Naturalism" "Technique"
Mumford	Disorder Interaction Inflexibility

Drawing heavily on the implications of the rough models shown above, and considering as important many of the ideas expressed by various authors earlier in this section, I have designed what might be called a Cyclic-Entropic Developmental Model which, I think, can be applied to individual journalists, to individual media, and to media systems. If there is validity in this hypothesis (and I am *not trying to prove it* at present), it does suggest a very bleak and pessimistic future for the existential journalist. Perhaps it is even bleaker for the non-existential journalist for he will adjust to it without even realizing the corroding influence on his Self which it will bring. So, in view of the discussion which has just preceded, I shall present the following chart (on the next page) without further comment.

From Pessimism to Pragmatic Freedom

After reading the preceding sections with their themes of pessimism, anxiety, and the illness besetting free journalism, the reader may wonder how the journalist can continue to feel a challenge as he looks to the future. It is, admittedly, a chilling and dismal outlook, and the average (non-existential) journalist actually does not feel much challenge. He has settled into a comfortable, cooperative niche in order to avoid the frightening implications of the journalistic future just described. He thinks he will live peaceably and harmoniously with the institutions that increasingly subsume him, and in this way he can achieve the greatest happiness for himself.

The existential journalist, on the other hand, recognizing (and *persistently* recognizing) the constantly restricting freedom that surrounds him, takes this "dismal" future as a challenge, as the *normal* state, something to be lived in dynamically and actively;

Cyclic-Entropic Model of Journalism

BIRTH-CHILDHOOD "SPRINGTIME" -------->	YOUTH "SUMMER" -------->	MATURITY "AUTUMN" -------->	OLD AGE/DEATH "WINTER" -------->
Authoritarianism	Authoritarianism Libertarianism	Libertarianism Authoritarianism	Authoritarianism
Tribalism-Groupism Tight Organization Fatalism Conformity-Stability-Conservatism Harmony-Growing Energy	Autocracy Relaxed Organization Experimentation Conformity-Stability-Conservatism Harmony-Growing Energy	Democracy-Individualism Optimism-Complacency Non-Conformity-Liberalism Disharmony	Statism-Collectivism Tight Organization Fatalism-Passivity Conformity-Stability-Conservatism Harmony- Decreasing Energy
"Primitive" "Prehistoric" >----------->	"Humanist" "Promethean-Faustian" "Historic" >------------>	"New Middle Ages" >------------>	"Ascetic" "Posthistoric" >----------->
TRADITIONAL >----------->	TRANSITIONAL >------------>	EARLY MODERN MODERN >----------->	LATE MODERN
Personal-Oral Media Informal and Rather Dull Interpersonal Communication "Elite Media" Simple-Scarce Cooperative-Monolithic	Print-Electronic	Electronic-Print More Formal Institutional Media Mass & Specialized Media Mixed-Bountiful Adversary-Pluralistic	Electronic-Print Automation Media Highly Institutionalized Very Formal Structure Media as Control Agents Simple-Mixed-Electronic Cooperative-Monolithic

he sees it as an invitation to combat, to fight against the encirclement of the system, to plunge into the tumultuous waters of journalism and flail out at the monstrous waves of conformism and depersonalization. The pessimistic future—or the existential journalist's consciousness of it—is what spurs him to persistent and courageous action. Gain as much freedom, be as original and creative, write as intensively and vigorously, as possible; relate to the journalistic problems courageously, and exercise the maximum autonomy or self-determination: this is the imperative of the existential journalist. Instead of retiring from the struggle because of the danger of it, or because of the meaninglessness of it all, or because of the gloomy future that lies ahead, the existential journalist takes all of this as an inspiration and a stimulus to live a more intensive life.

The existential journalist cares little about theoretical freedom. He is concerned about *living*—acting out—his freedom. He is dedicated to creating Norbert Wiener's "islands of decreasing entropy" where the authentic self can breathe freely as it pushes constantly into the future, gaining essence or substantial nature as it goes. He knows that to be a *true* journalist or a real person he must be an individualist—even a non-conformist.

Emerson's words pound instinctively in his ears: "Who would be a man, must be a nonconformist. He who would gather immortal palms must not be hindered by the name of goodness, but must explore if it be goodness. Nothing is at last sacred but the integrity of your own mind. Absolve you to yourself, and you shall have the suffrage of the world."[73] And here again, are words of Emerson which stir the existentialist spirit:

> Let us affront and reprimand the smooth mediocrity and squalid contentment of the times. . . . Man is timid and apologetic; he is no longer upright; he dares not say, "I think," "I am," but quotes some saint or sage. He is ashamed before the blade of grass or the blowing rose. . . . Insist on yourself; never imitate. . . . Every great man is unique. . . . Nothing can bring you peace but yourself. Nothing can bring you peace but the triumph of principles.[74]

Of course, the existential journalist knows that absolute and unconditional freedom is an abstraction; but he also knows, that

---

[73] From "Self Reliance," quoted in Raymond Van Over, *The Psychology of Freedom* (Greenwich, Conn.: Fawcett Premier Books, 1974), p. 112.

[74] *Ibid.*, pp. 118-36 *passim*.

within the wide limits granted to individual willing, he can make many decisions and exercise a tremendous amount of freedom. He knows that he must be free in order to be ethical, or to be "responsible." The existential journalist knows that he can always refuse to do something, to write some story, to interview some person, to change some headline. He can always say No, which for Sartre is the ultimate and final freedom that cannot be taken away.[75] But the temptation is ever before the journalist to evade such decisions and to "go along" with the system, taking orders and doing things which eh really does not want to do. As Karl Jaspers puts it:

> Man would like to be able to renounce himself, to plunge into his work as into the waters of oblivion, to be no longer free but merely "natural."[76]

But, according to Jaspers, the existential journalist can not so renounce himself and escape from his real being. Only can a journalist come to his own self, according to Jaspers, if he experiences "the harshness of the real" and plays an active part in the world—even though he aims at "an impossible, an unattainable goal." This, says Jaspers, is the "necessary pre-condition of one's own being."[77]

Nikolai Berdyaev writes of freedom as the autonomy of man, and as a love of truth, a concept which is compatible with the press libertarian (e.g., John Stuart Mill) belief that freedom of expression presents the best chance for truth to emerge. Berdyaev writes:

> Man is a slave because freedom is difficult, whereas slavery is easy.... The free man is simply the man who does not allow the alientation, the ejection into the external of his conscience and his judgment. He who permits this is a slave. The master also permits it, but he is only another form of slave.... It is the autonomy of man, as personality, that must be called freedom.... The free man is a self-governing being not a governed being.... Truth is always connected with freedom and bestowed upon freedom only. Slavery is always the denial of truth and the dread of truth.[78]

The journalist often responds to words of this nature with

---

[75] Barrett, *Irrational Man*, p. 241.
[76] Jaspers, *Man in the Modern Age*, p. 181.
[77] *Ibid.*, p. 197.
[78] Quoted in Van Over, pp. 227-28.

"How idealistic! How naive! How unreasonable! These people don't understand the realities of working for a newspaper!" It is a truism in journalism that one can't do his "own thing," that he must follow directions, conform to the editorial policy, etc. And this rationalization is always standing by, ready to be used by journalists as they live largely in Sartrean "bad faith" in their work. Sartre and other existentialists have been aware of the difficulty of being free. Each journalist, in spite of difficulties and dangers, has the freedom *to try* to accomplish his ends. As Sartre points out, "we cannot say that a prisoner is always free to go out of prison, which would be absurd . . . but that he is always free to try to escape."[79] And, as he says in another place, "the formula 'to be free' does not mean 'to obtain what one has wished' but rather 'by oneself to determine oneself to wish' (in the broad sense of choosing)."[80] And, if the journalist does not *will himself to be free* (even if he fails), he chooses the inauthentic life; for he must, as Carl Jaspers says, "on his initiative independently gain possession of the mechanism of his life, or else, himself degraded to become a machine, surrender to the apparatus."[81]

*   *   *

So, we see that the existential journalist prizes free acts. These, of course, have consequences, and the existential journalist must take these into consideration when making his decisions. For he is responsible for the consequences coming from his free acts, whether or not he anticipated them. He must stand behind his acts, his decisions, and must not give excuses or plead inability to go against orders. For he can always say *no* to orders. Peter Koestenbaum writes that responsibility for all of a person's action is uniquely his. The experience of responsibility, he says, is a constant reminder that his actions are his, that he is an individual, and that nothing can change that fact.[82] And, writing of consequences of actions, and a person's responsibility for them, he says:

---

[79] Quoted in Robert C. Solomon (ed.), *Phenomenology and Existentialism* (New York: Harper & Row, 1972), p. 462.

[80] *Ibid.*; Cf., J.-P. Sartre, *Being and Nothingness* (New York: Philosophical Library, Inc., 1956).

[81] Jaspers, *Man in the Modern Age*, p. 195.

[82] Peter Koestenbaum, *Philosophy: A General Introduction* (New York: American Book Co., 1968), p. 324.

My involvement with the consequences of my action is neither a moral relation in the traditional sense, nor a sociological convention, nor a divine edict. That I am responsible for the consequences of my acts, because I initiated these and could have chosen otherwise—whether the consequences could have been foreseen or not—is merely the recognition of a fundamental and irrefutable *fact* of my nature and a *fact* about my experience of being human, disclosed by introspective phenomenological analysis.[83]

Many journalists fear freedom for the very reason that they fear to assume responsibility for their decision. For when a person assumes freedom he forces himself to throw off his inertia, cut himself loose from tradition, and, what is most important, he puts himself in a position of accepting moral responsibility for his actions. There is a reluctance for journalists to take this step toward freedom and responsibility. Here and there, now and then, some journalists do arise to the defense of freedom and speak out against the restrictions and limitations of the prevailing system. But often their solution, it is interesting to note, consists of an *organization* of journalists to do combat—a "profession" or a union or a society—instead of assuming individually a dedication to personal choice and action.

The struggle for autonomy, freedom, and authenticity in journalism is a personal struggle. In the face of a pessimistic future for journalism where conformity and depersonalization is growing and freedom is dying, the individual journalist must wage continuous and personal war against the beguiling pressures to conform. The journalist—if he is an existentialist—must be committed to protecting and expanding his individuality and to *taking action*, in the face of personal risk, to frustrate the forces which would enslave and depersonalize him.

---

[83] *Ibid.*

5

Individualism, Commitment, and Action

Human nature is not a machine to be built after a model, and set to do exactly the work prescribed for it, but a tree, which requires to grow and develop itself on all sides, according to the tendency of the inward forces which make it a living thing.

—JOHN STUART MILL, *On Liberty*

In every act of rebellion, the rebel simultaneously experiences a feeling of revulsion at the infringement of his rights and a complete and spontaneous loyalty to certain aspects of himself.

—ALBERT CAMUS, *The Rebel*

For, believe me, the secret of the greatest fruitfulness and the greatest enjoyment of existence is: to live *dangerously!* Build your cities under Vesuvius! Send your ships into uncharted seas! Live at war with your peers and yourselves!

—FRIEDRICH NIETZSCHE, *The Gay Science*

FAR TOO MANY JOURNALISTS cower in their corners of the newsroom, routinely making standard marks and pushing regular buttons, or trudge the noisy corridors of life like rusty robots set in perpetual and monotonous motion. They live only in the sense that they breathe, communicate only in the sense that they utter the expected platitudes, commit themselves only to their regularized duties, and act only in predictable and institutionalized ways designed to stabilize and harmonize.

These are harsh words. They are meant to be.

After more than a quarter of a century of dealing with journalists, journalism professors, and journalism students in most parts of the world, I am convinced that the great majority of them are devoid of a sense of self—of a sense of personal worth and unique potency; I am convinced that most go through their days contenting themselves with not rocking the boat, with not saying the "wrong" things, with not antagonizing those who might cause them harm or anxiety. Basically, most journalists are timid souls. They are devoid of individualism and authenticity and have found shelter in the safe coves of corporate journalism. They have rationalized their inauthentic existence by flying the insipid banners of group loyalty and institutional cooperation. "Harmony" is their theme song. "Cooperation" is their life's strategy. An unwillingness to individual commitment and a fear of putting themselves in positions of personal danger have led the typical modern journalists down the road to self-stagnation. Journalism today has, by and large, become a world of purring machines, operated by machine-like functionaries, harmoniously packaging standardized news and mass-approved opinion.

Individualism is disdained in the average news operation. The eccentric, the person with integrity, with a mind of his own, is being squeezed out of journalism. He is looked upon increasingly, by his superiors and his colleagues and co-workers, as a poor "team person," one who does not fit nicely into the corporate journalistic system. The journalist with his own ideas, his own sense of moral values, his own strict standards of language usage, his own journalistic philosophy—if you will—is looked on with suspicion, or even hostility.

This state of affairs has several causes. One, of course, is the natural inclination of human beings to "escape from freedom" and from the traumatic experiences which often come from exercising one's own choices and accepting responsibility for them. Another is the growing specialization in journalism which, naturally, decreases the individual's dependence on himself and pressures him to put increased faith in the total cooperative effort. And another cause, to be discussed further in the next chapter, is the system of education which tends to package neo-journalists in conventional ways so that they will be more acceptable in the status-quo, conservative world of American journalism. And, finally and perhaps most importantly, is the growing inclination of individual persons in journalism to give up their individuality of their own volition, to retreat into the corporate structure for financial and psychological reasons, and to conform to inauthentic practices which sap their being of individuality.

Individualism: In Pursuit of Self

The existential journalist rebels against the dismal picture painted above. He is determined that, in the midst of this situation where depersonalizing pressures are growing ever more powerful, he will retain a substantial amount of his individuality. And, it is this determination on the part of the existential journalist which assures him of success. He *wants* to keep his personhood; he is *committed* to keeping it; he *acts* in such ways as to keep it: therefore, he will keep it. Of course, it may be painful to him in many ways, but he has the sweet satisfaction of knowing that he has retained his integrity, his unique essence, his individual self.

Kierkegaard in his *The Present Age* criticized his society, and proved to be very prophetic; for this essay has been the source of much existentialist criticism of modern society; such recent books as David Riesman's *The Lonely Crowd* and William Whyte's *The Organization Man* are still repeating and documenting his insights.

The individual is dying, Kierkegaard pointed out; there is a drift toward mass society, and this means the death of the individual as life grows more and more collectivized and externalized. Increasingly, he says, the social thinking is being determined by what William Barrett has called the Law of Large Numbers.[1] Karl Jaspers relates this idea to journalism, noting that when the journalist performs his work day after day in a routine way, he sinks "into the fathomless abysses of oblivion."[2] And, of course, it is very easy for him to sink into such oblivion in the typical corporate journalistic medium. He works for a modern large corporation or organization, which as John Gardner notes, loves and promotes "stability," not efficiency.[3] With this natural tendency of journalistic media toward stability, a kind of mediocrity develops, and functionaries become ever more the "same" or equal. Mediocrity breeds mediocrity, Gardner has pointed out,

---

[1] *Irrational Man*, p. 173.

[2] *Man in the Modern Age*, p. 204.

[3] John W. Gardner, *Excellence* (New York: Harper & Row—Perennial Library, 1971), p. 31.

and organizations and labor unions protect their "least able members."[4] In fact, oftentimes it is quite obvious that organizations take a kind of pride in, and give various kinds of rewards to, their mediocre members rather than superior ones who pose some kind of threat (at least psychological) to all others concerned.

Any observant and thinking person, looking at the world of journalism, must be struck by the increasing conformity, the growing mechanization and regimentation, the submission of the individual journalist to an ever-growing number of authorities—in short, journalism is increasingly subsuming the individual. "He is drowned in the mass," says Jacques Ellul, "and becomes convinced that he is only a cipher and that he really cannot be considered otherwise in such a large number of individuals."[5] When one looks beneath the patina of "busyness" of the average newsroom, he is struck by the smileless faces, the over-serious demeanor of men and women going through unenthusiastic activities devoid of a spirit of vitality and creativity.

"The individual feels himself *diminished*," says Ellul. "For one thing, he gets the feeling that he is under constant supervision and can never exercise his independent initiative; for another, he thinks he is always being pushed down to a lower level."[6] And, Carl Jung notes that "individual judgment grows increasingly uncertain of itself. . . , responsibility is collectivized as much as possible, i.e., is shuffled off by the individual and delegated to a corporate body."[7] Very few journalists go against such regimentation, such collectivized conformity; very few of them heed Thoreau's words to let their lives "be a counter-friction to stop the machine."[8]

The pressure, the temptation, is strong for the individual journalist to follow a kind of "spirit of consensus," to give in to numbers. But the existential journalist strives constantly to follow Gabriel Marcel's admonition to reject "the fascination of numbers" so that he "can hope to remain at the spiritual level, that is, at the level of truth."[9] Nietzsche was certainly one who

---

[4] *Ibid.*, pp. 17-33 *passim.*

[5] *Propaganda* (New York: Vintage Books, 1973), p. 149.

[6] *Ibid.*

[7] *Undiscovered Self*, p. 26.

[8] From "Civil Disobedience" in Carl Bode (ed.) *The Portable Thoreau* (New York: Viking Press, 1947), p. 120.

[9] *Man Against Mass Society* (Chicago: Henry Regnery Co.—a Gateway Edition, 1969), p. 221.

recognized the accelerating trend toward the loss of the individual's importance; individualism was dying, he believed, and he felt that he should present the world with the heroic figure of his *Uebermensch*, his spiritual Superman. Like Nietzsche, Kierkegaard was troubled by the spread of "herd mentality." The two philosophers agree that the individual is being emptied of all value and engulfed in some organization, corporation, institution, or some dominant totality. Kierkegaard calls the typical person a "cipher-man" or a "fractional man," having his purpose and importance not in himself but only in a quantitative social whole.[10]

The existential journalist, the committed and active journalist, will daily seek his own individuality in the face of the obstacles noted above. He will strive for individual fulfillment in the very fact of fighting such obstacles, although he realizes that it is highly unlikely (or impossible) that individual fulfillment for many (on a large scale) will ever be achieved. For large-scale individual fulfillment would have to assume a radically different social system than is known at present. As John Gardner says:

> Individual fulfillment on a wide scale can occur only in a society which is designed to cherish the individual, which has the strength to protect him, and richness and diversity to stimulate and develop him, and the system of values within which he can find himself—and lose himself!—as a person.[11]

While achieving a wide-spread or universal journalistic capacity for self-fulfillment, there is, of course, the opportunity for existential minorities to individualize themselves. It is a matter of *willing*. It is a matter of the journalist desiring to be himself— or better, constantly and authentically *to create* himself. As Sartre points out: "You are nothing else than your life."[12] One of the chief reasons for a loss of personhood and individuality is a drift toward non-action, toward a kind of passive, non-involved state. Sartre says that the existentialist must involve himself and act on the old saw, "Nothing ventured, nothing gained."[13] When the journalist ventures, when he forces or wills himself to be himself, to take actions, he reestablishes and reinforces his own

---

[10] James Collins, *The Mind of Kierkegaard* (Chicago: Henry Regnery Co.—a Gateway Edition, 1967), p. 184.

[11] Gardner, p. 173.

[12] Jean-Paul Sartre, *Existentialism and Human Emotions* (New York: Philosophical Library—Wisdom Library, 1957), p. 33.

[13] *Ibid.*, p. 31.

individuality. When he stops, when he passively floats along, when he ceases *willing* and acting, his individuality slips away and he becomes inauthentic as a person.

Style: a Revelation of Self

The journalist who desires to be an individual, who wants to be as authentic as possible, will naturally push himself in that direction. He will endeavor to be himself as much as possible within the obvious limits which journalism as a social institution permits. One of the most obvious evidences of increasing individuality is the *style* of the journalist. When a journalist cherishes his uniqueness, he also cherishes, develops, and protects his journalistic style, most obvious in his writing and, in the case of broadcast journalism, his speaking and "microphone personality."

Style is personal. It is the highly individualized dimension in journalism. It is through style that one's personhood breaks through; it is a revelation of one's self. The tendency is, in the evolving journalistic corporate institution, to hide one's style, to cover it up, to submerge it under a blanket of anonymity and conformity. But style is important and the journalist who loses it—or never has the real opportunity to develop it—commits a kind of journalistic suicide. He can, by treasuring and refining his style, strengthen his personhood. For, in effect, he *is* his style. Therefore, a negation of style indicates a negation of self.

Just as the existential journalist wants to *live* authentically, he also wants to evidence this existential dimension in the style of his journalism. He pushes as far as he can with his individualized linguistic probes; he gets himself into his written and spoken messages to the fullest extent. He opposes as vigorously as possible the concept of journalistic "neutrality" and dispassionate communication.

As the existential journalist's horizons change and broaden, so will his writing style; as he changes and makes himself, he is also making his style. He takes chances and experiments in his total life-acts, thereby manifesting his total "style" or personality; in the same way he must evidence commitment in his communication style. Flexibility of style is an imperative for him. He changes; his style changes. He is his style—or, his style indicates his truest nature or essence.

To change, to improve his style, the journalist must, first of all, seriously desire to change it. By wanting to change it, he evidences a fundamental desire to change himself, to push toward the future, to create himself anew—in short, to live existentially. He must change many of his normal habits and thrust himself into new environments—physical and intellectual. He must read carefully and critically, noting stylistic techniques which he grafts creatively onto his own writing. He must become conscious of other (and fresh) points of view, not necessarily to embrace them, but to use them, to benefit from them, to adapt them, to use them as catalysts to his own thought and imagination.

It is at this point that the journalist begins to change his style of writing—as he changes his *attitude* toward life and toward communicating this through his language. He has new ideas and impressions to structure, or to integrate with his old ones. The past style flows into the present and into the future; he has developed a dynamic style that changes as he changes—and, possibly, as the situation changes. As the existential journalist renews himself, so is his journalistic style renewed.

He sees new vistas, he hears strange voices, he receives different sensations, he contemplates unfamiliar ideas. He tries new techniques, he experiments with new forms, he pushes his ideas into new regions of thought; in short, he begins a new psychological and linguistic life and feels fresh intellectual winds in his face. As his horizons change and broaden, he breaks out of his confining prison of provincial and trite patterns of thought and action; he steps into a new verbal world, which, in addition to making his life richer and more satisfying, offers the verbal freedom necessary for the development of an existential style proper to a freedom-loving, authentic personhood.

Style can be honest. Honesty is an important aspect of authenticity and individuality. If a journalist's style is to reflect the authenticity of the journalist, it *must* be honest—meaning that it must spring from an unpolluted and pure Self. Style is the dimension of journalism that gives it power, individuality, variety, and charm. In a sense it is verbal magic. If the person is authentic, he will reflect this in his style; this existential style will manifest itself in language that makes a word sparkling, a sentence unforgettable, a passage stimulating, an article impelling and meaningful.

F. L. Lucas, long-time Cambridge don and teacher of writing, has said that the writer must (1) respect truth and himself, and (2) respect his readers.[14] These two facets of respect, as Lucas sees them, evidence the writer's honesty and courtesy and are cornerstones of good style. The implications here are significant. The journalist, in order to have a good style, must present his true self, however unpleasant it might be. He must be honest with himself and with his reader; pretense will find him out. Or, at least, he will find his own dishonesty out—and it will dissolve his authenticity. Honest style is really difficult to achieve—as is, of course, basic honesty—for the temptation is great to be eccentric, to be inauthentically impressive or profound—or, even worse perhaps, to avoid portions of the truth which might pain the journalist or someone else.

Honest style is style that is consistent with the journalist's being. It is style that participates not in hypocrisy nor delusion, but furnishes an appropriate (reliable) dress for the existential self.

If the journalist is a cliché himself, he will have a style that is cliché-ridden. The existential journalist will rebel against clichés just as he rebels against any influence that tends to depersonalize him and take away the stamp of his special, individual self. When one uses clichés, he escapes from himself; he loses himself in the vague, generalized and fuzzy forests of linguistic universals. He hides his real self—his real style—in Everyman's language. This is not the way of the existential journalist. He follows Thoreau's advice to be "resolutely and faithfully" what he is and what he aspires to be.[15]

The existential journalist, first and foremost, wants what might be called an "open" style. Openness is very important in authentic communication. Jaspers has called this "open level" of communication *Daseinkommunikation*; only through this honest and forthright communication can one recognize *Existenz*. Jaspers says it "involves complete openness, unqualified renunciation of the uses of power and advantage, and concerns the other's self-realization as fully as one's own."[16] The journalist as communicator is never quite sure that what he is signifying in his messages is truly what he wishes to signify, or—as Sartre adds—

---

[14] *Holiday*, XXVII (March 1960), pp. 11ff.

[15] *Thoreau on Man and Nature*, a compilation of writings from Thoreau by A. D. Volkman (Mt. Vernon, N.Y.: The Peter Pauper Press, 1960), p. 13.

[16] Hanno Hardt, "The Dilemma of Mass Communications: An Existential Point of View," *Philosophy & Rhetoric*, Vol. 5, No. 3 (Pennsylvania State University), 179.

if he is "signifying anything."[17] In spite of this constant communication anxiety, the existential journalist must try, and keep on trying. He must be "open" and honest. In order to develop an authentic style, one which he hopes will deepen the communication, the journalist needs first to be himself, to owe his allegiance to his personhood, to drop all pretense and affectation in his language, to let his own character and personality show through in his style. This is really quite simple, but it demands courage and a sincere desire to escape from the incapsulating world of conformist thought, action, and language that dominate in most mass media. One must, of course, adapt one's style to the particular situation and circumstance—letting one aspect of style dominate here, another there—but the core, the foundation, of one's style is manifest in all of the existential journalist's work.

The main key, I suppose, is that the journalist must develop a greater respect for himself, have confidence in himself as a person and a journalist, come to the recognition that he has ideas and a manner of expression which are just as important and as individualistic as those of any other person, free himself from the temptation to cling too closely to the general way of doing journalism, and experiment with new ideas and practices as often as possible. The need is for the journalist to launch into his own verbal universe! This is really a psychological problem, and only when the journalist has wrestled with it, and conquered it, will he become himself, and will be free to develop a truly individual style.

Daring to "let oneself go" and to experiment, and to cast old concepts in new ways: this is the most important consideration in style. In 1971 I was asked to write a "journalist's creed." Actually I am not overly impressed with creeds and codes of ethics, and the like, thinking them generally useless and trite, but I accepted the assignment, "let myself go," and came up with one which, admittedly, has many weaknesses. But it does show that journalism creeds do not have to be all alike. My creed, presented below, was beautifully set in type by Thomas Bell, a printer at the University of Missouri School of Journalism; he liked the message of the creed and wanted to make copies available. This creed will, I think, say something about individualism, and about style in itself. So, I present it here without comment:

---

[17] *Being and Nothingness* (New York: Philosophical Library, 1956), p. 373.

(A JOURNALIST'S CREED)
DEDICATION TO *Language*

I dedicate myself to words —
    words that spill like flimsy fish
    through the nets of understanding;
    I would become a net-repairer,
    or build new nets of tougher fiber;
    I would constrain the elusive words
    that flash shimmering before the eyes
    and flirt with the mind.

I turn away from weak, wet words
    that wash away at the edges,
    and flop their frigid forms in sad gesture.
    I seek the precise words, the firm words,
    words that pierce to the inner core
    of consciousness with meaning and knowledge.
    I relish those words that alternately growl and purr
    as they rush to do my bidding.

I dedicate myself to language —
    to language that fits the occasion,
    to words that roll to the cadence of the message
    and spark the flames of excitement.

I dedicate myself to verbal precision
    that cuts cleanly through the thickened thought
    and seeks the crystal core of credibility.

I eschew the charred word,
    the undernourished and overused word,
    the weary word
    that flays away at thoughtless minds
    and drones drearily in dark redundance.

I seek words that grab the truth
    and cast it courageously before the crowd,
    intent always on directness and light,
    avoiding the dank darkness of delusion.

In sum, I dedicate myself
    to harness and use that ponderous pounding
    of language that restlessly rolls across
    the barrier reefs of perception
    and persistently probes
    the shifting beaches of humanity.

— JOHN MERRILL
1971

*   *   *

The existential journalist will have a style which is part poetic and part scientific. Like the poet, he must have a "feeling" for language and a desire to make something vivid and meaningful with his language patterns. He must learn, like the poet, to make his sentences say just as much as possible, and he must describe people and objects in the light of his own feeling about them. As the poet, he must try to create something that goes beyond pure objective description; the writer must add the other dimension of *self*, which largely manifests itself in journalistic style. The existential journalist is, probably, more a poet than a scientist, but he has some concern for the scientific approach.

He, at least, has a strain of the scientific concern running through him, but this will be kept well under control and used only to enhance the personalistic dimension of his work. Like the scientist, he will keep an open mind—at least a flexible one which will admit new data, however disconcerting, through the doors of his mind. He must attempt always to be fair, to be thorough, to be sensitive to differences while recognizing the value of categories and generalizations. Like the scientist, the existential journalist is an adventurer, an explorer—filled with curiosity and a desire to capture as much of reality as possible for himself and his audiences. He must be curious about what is over that proverbial next hill; this curiosity projects him *personally* over the next hill. He is really not satisfied to *hear* about what is over there; he must go and see for himself. He tries to get as close to reality as possible; he is dissatisfied with second-hand accounts, with quoting others—this is for the non-existential journalists. The existential journalist is a reality-confronter; he is not a dispassionate stenographer of life. He is a plunger-in; he wants to go and see, not to sit and listen. He is a "news-getter," not a "news-reporter." Or at least he puts his main emphasis on the "getting," the "immersing" in reality—and "reporting" or communicating this reality in a meaningful way is a by-product.

This is quite a different journalistic orientation from the more common non-existential one. In it, *reporting* and all other kinds of "sending" of messages is what is important: in other words, the *communication* is the significant thing, with the emphasis on the message. With the existentialist, while the message is certainly important, the emphasis is upon the *journalist* and his true involvement with the reality of his story. Certainly, the process of communicating this involvement cannot be denied, but it is not the major concern of the existential journalist.

Involvement, commitment, plunging into the reality of the story give authenticity to the journalist's account—and by projection give it its *real* meaning. These are the qualities which humanize the story, give it a dimension of significance on a truly human level. Dispassionate and "objective" journalism is for someone else—not the existential journalist. Objective journalism—a kind of neutral orientation, sublimates the journalist's authentic self, and signifies the death of "style." Perhaps we should consider more closely this whole matter of subjectivity and objectivity in journalism.

Subjectivity: Its Place in Journalism

The existential journalist has a deep-rooted respect for subjectivity; this is natural, for he actually "thinks about" the nature of reality and the ways it can best be communicated. He knows that the normal sense of "objectivity" enthroned by most journalists is suspect; he instinctively—and intellectually—knows that objective journalism goes beyond what is usually considered "objective"—beyond the "accurate quotes," the "correct" spellings of names, the highly selective bits of information which purport to "tell the story." He *knows* that factually correct stories do not comprise objectivity. He is convinced that neutrality and dispassionate writing do not assure objectivity in a story. He is aware, of course, that he does not really know himself what objective journalism is, but he is sure that it has aspects and subtleties not present in the highly regarded journalistic concept of reportorial "neutrality."

He agrees with Michael Novak when he says that so-called "objective reporting" leads to misunderstandings in American journalism, and something is needed beyond "merely objective or neutral reporting."[18] Novak recommends what he calls a "largeness of mind and soul" for reporters; this, he emphasizes, is "quite different from pretended objectivity." He points out, too, that "there are no facts 'out there' apart from human

---

[18] Michael Novak, *The Experience of Nothingness* (New York: Harper Colophon Books, 1971), p. 39.

observers" and that these human observers (reporters) become "not more, but less astute when they try to be neutral."[19]

Novak insists that a more adequate sense of reality must be established which will take us beyond the old idea of reportorial neutrality and lack of passion. The first step in developing this more adequate sense of reality, he suggests, "is to recognize that objectivity is a psychological state,"[20] that it requires the cultivation of specific subjective states, the disciplining of attention and selected thought habits, the selection of one set of values in preference to others, and the shaping of perception and other mental operations. The journalist's sense of reality is gratified, says Novak, when he thinks of himself as being neutral or "objective," when he has what he considers the "hard facts," when "the figures" are all there in front of him. For instance, in Vietnam the journalists constantly provided us with *numbers*; they counted dead and wounded, missing in action, miles of road, telephones, airplanes, doctors, and on and on. But, asks Novak, did all this "objectivity" in the form of "hard facts"—numbers—assure the journalists (or their audiences) a good grasp of Vietnamese reality?

Existentialists such as Buber, Tillich, Sartre, and Heidegger have attacked the emptiness of empirical, pragmatic objectivity so beloved by American journalists. They have said that this sense of reality is too matter-of-fact, automatic, and functional—and that such a concept of objectivity causes a loss of admiration for the human person.[21] H. L. Mencken, a tough-minded American reporter, was in agreement with this basic philosophical perspective of Novak, but he couched his observations on objectivity in more straightforward journalistic language:

> Newspaper men like to think of news as something wholly objective, but it can be so only under exceptional circumstances. In its ordinary forms it is not merely a statement of overt facts; it is some concrete individual's opinion of the truth and significance of those facts. He may try in all honesty to keep his customary prejudices out of it, but nine times out of ten they creep in, nevertheless. . . . It is, in truth, this admixture of opinion which gives good reporting all its savor.[22]

---

[19] *Ibid.*
[20] *Ibid.*, p. 37.
[21] *Ibid.*, p. 36.
[22] Mencken, *A Gang of Pecksniffs*, pp. 182-83.

According to Mencken, the reader wants this admixture of the reporter's observations, interpretation, and opinion in order to receive a "clear and vivid picture." The reporter provides this, according to Mencken, by working his view into the story, and "by illuminating that report with whatever wisdom he may have at his command."[23] For, says Mencken, "he can see only through his own eyes, and can weigh conflicting evidence only in the balance of his own judgment."[24] This idea is presented by Novak as the good reporter's "walking around events," in such a way as to show us "more than one interpretation of them, using his own skills as an interpreter to portray deep and subtle nuances of various points of view."[25]

The term "subjectivity" is normally treated by American journalists as if it were anathema to good reporting. And, perhaps, the modern dignification of "science" is largely responsible for this idea—for science is "objective" and everything else is "subjective"; science gets at the truth, and everything else does not. Hwa Yol Jung, writing on existentialism and phenomenology, deals with this point:

> The affirmation of objectivism to the exclusion of subjectivism is misleading because it ignores the place of subjectivity in thought and observation. What is observable (a datum), for example, is always related to the awareness of an observer. A datum of observation is not yet a fact, and a fact is meaningful only in relation to the observer for whom it is a fact. Thus a fact is nothing but meaning given to a datum (or data) by the observer in the process of observation. Further, the truth of a fact or thought for one observer is sanctioned intersubjectively—that is, by a scientific or intellectual community. As consciousness is intentional, reflect thought, whether philosophical or scientific, is neither entirely subjective nor entirely objective.[26]

Very often has the journalist heard such words as these from an editor or colleague: "Is it correct? Did the source really say that? Is his name spelled correctly? Are you sure he lives at that address?" This sort of questioning in regard to a story might be considered a kind of journalistic substantiation of objectivity. Seldom are these types of questions asked: "In what context did

---

[23] *Ibid.*, p. 183.

[24] *Ibid.*

[25] Novak, *Experience of Nothingness*, p. 40.

[26] Hwa Yol Jung, (ed.), *Existential Phenomenology and Political Theory: A Reader* (Chicago: Henry Regnery Co., 1972), p. xxvi.

he say that? What *else* did he say? Was he smiling when he said that? Did he really mean this or was it an off-the-cuff remark or joke? Is what he said really true?" These are the questions which seek to get beneath the normal journalistic concept of objectivity; they are usually not asked because they are hard to answer—and they force the reporter into a completely different level of reporting. They force him to think, to judge, to form opinions, to interpret, to attempt to give a "total context" kind of report. And they force him to get himself into the story. He is accustomed to giving bits and pieces of the event, strung together in rather juvenile paragraphs of one-or-two-sentences. His main concern is usually with what is merely "correct" (and even this he cannot handle too well), not with what is contextually true. And there is a difference.

Karl Jaspers warns that we need to be dissatisfied with "what is merely correct," and points out that often the truth is obscured by "a variety of opinions which are hung on the skeleton of a supposedly rational pattern."[27] Truth, according to Jaspers, is "infinitely *more* than scientific correctness."[28] What the existential journalist will seek, I suppose, is what Jaspers calls an "Encompassing." He distinguishes this from the objective, the particular, the accurate, the purely factual. It is a *larger truth*, a greater "objectivity" which has real significance and meaning. It is close to what William Stephenson has called *factuality* reporting, in contrast to *fact* reporting—a kind of reporting which tries to get at the "essence" of an event.[29] The existential journalist will be dissatisfied with merely reporting the "facts," selected and presented out of context and in a meaningless, unsynthesized, superficial manner.

This *Encompassing* of Jaspers, this *factuality* of Stephenson is similar to the German *Faktizitat* (facticity); it goes beyond what is simply "observed," and has to do with the inward, existential awareness. In journalism it would include more than surface description; it would deal with motivations, psychological states, feelings, etc. that would escape most journalistic reports. This *facticity*, as applied to journalism, has to do with

---

[27] "Existenzphilosophie" in Walter Kaufmann (ed.), *Existentialism from Dostoevsky to Sartre* (New York: New American Library—Meridian Books, 1975), p. 175.

[28] *Ibid*.

[29] John C. Merrill, *The Imperative of Freedom* (New York: Hastings House, 1974), p. 154.

basic, fundamental aspects of persons and situations which are usually not considered important enough, or interesting enough to report—or, with the part which is deemed beyond the understanding of the reporter.

The existential reporter, however, will try to get at these aspects of the story. *What* a person is differs from *who* he is (a surface journalistic fact); the *what* includes the why—and a concern with this aspect gets the journalist to another level of journalistic expression. Facticity reporting, then, for the existential journalist focuses on the "state of being there," a kind of total context presentation, in a certain situation; the reporter must try to see everything from the perspective of the situation. In reporting a speech, for example, the journalist must not simply quote the *words* of the speaker, provide an outward description of the speaker, give the identification of the speaker, but he must try to "get into" the speaker's mind, to present his motivations, his feelings, and he must try to go beyond the actual words to an interpretation of facial expressions, gestures, raised eyebrows, smiles, etc. Also he must not forget the environment of the speech, the conditions under which the person is speaking, the audience and its reactions. A speech story, in other words, is far more than a stenographic record of the words a speaker utters.

Although it is contrary to most American journalistic practice and to most teaching in journalism schools, the concept of good reporting must also stress the *feelings* of the reporter. Usually the reporter is admonished to keep himself—most certainly his "feelings"—out of his story, but sometimes these feelings of the reporter are very important. As John Macquarrie says, the feelings are not necessarily "antithetical to reason and thought"; in fact, he says, they are "a source of insights."[30] Through his feeling, his sensing, his premonitions, and hunches, the journalist has a "uniquely direct way of participating in the world"; his feelings or emotions are a kind of register of his "being-in-the-world."[31] Often, these "feelings" subjectivize a journalist's report even when he is unaware of it. They influence, for example, his selecting a "story" to report in the first place, and

---

[30] John Macquarrie, *Existentialism*, p. 119.

[31] Martin Heidegger speaks of *Gestimmtheit*—being "attuned" to the world; Paul Ricoeur uses a similar metaphor when he speaks of *tonalité*, as if one had to adjust to the "pitch" of the world. See Macquarrie, *Existentialism*, pp. 119-23 *passim*.

they cause him to choose various parts of it, and to organize and emphasize and "play" this selected information in certain ways. In the words of Karl Mannheim, the journalist "imposes a pattern on reality which reality itself does not have when we 'report' or describe it."[32] This is a pattern which Mannheim sees as "a projection of our own interests or assumptions and not of the facts themselves."[33]

Erich Fromm is insistent that "subjectivity" is important in reporting. *True* objectivity, as Fromm discusses it in *Man for Himself*, requires more than simply seeing an event or object dispassionately and neutrally; it requires the observer to become related in some way to that which is being reported. The nature of the object and the nature of the observer must be merged and considered equally important if we are to get at what constitutes true objectivity.[34] Fromm goes on to say that

> . . . objectivity is not, as it is often implied in a false idea of "scientific" objectivity, synonymous with detachment, with absence of interest and care. How can one penetrate the veiling surface of things to their causes and relationships if one does not have an interest that is vital and sufficiently impelling for so laborious a task?

Fromm stresses that objectivity does not mean detachment; rather he says, it has more to do with "respect." And he points out that the idea that lack of interest is a condition for recognizing the truth is fallacious. All productive thinking and observing and communicating are stimulated by the interest of the observer, according to Fromm. And it would seem that productive journalism, or journalism that reaches furthest toward *true* objectivity, would also be that which involves the interest of the reporter. It is impossible for the journalist to detach himself from his story if he is to give an honest and full ("encompassing") account. For as Fromm says, "To be able to listen to oneself is a prerequisite for the ability to listen to others; to be at home with oneself is the necessary condition for relating oneself to others."[35]

[32] Charles Frankel, *The Case for Modern Man*, pp. 134-35.

[33] Quotation from Frankel, p. 135. Cf. Karl Mannheim, *Ideology and Utopia* (New York: Harcourt, Brace & Co., 1936).

[34] *Man for Himself: An Inquiry into the Psychology of Ethics* (New York: Holt, Rinehart & Winston—Fawcett Premier Books, 1966), p. 111.

[35] *Ibid.*, p. 113. This idea is reinforced by Michael Novak in his *Belief and Unbelief: A Philosophy of Self-Knowledge* (New York: Mentor-Omega Books, 1965). Understanding, he points out, assumes intelligent subjectivity.

Now, someone may object, "But what about facts? Are not facts undistorted and objective reflections of reality?" Facts in themselves, as we have seen, have little correspondence to objectivity. Often they distort and mislead. A fact, says Fromm, presented "merely descriptively" may make the audience member more or less informed, and "it is well known that there is no more effective way of distortion than to offer nothing but a series of 'facts.' "[36] Pictures—in a sense visual "facts," too—can distort, whether they are "still" shots in the print media or filmed or live shots on television. Philip Wylie has expressed well, in spite of his cynical tone, this point:

> . . . it is claimed that TV has made a greater number of Americans better acquainted with more truth than they were in pre-TV days. Nothing could be less correct. More people doubtless have a slanted half-glimpse of more events, ideas, so-called scientific marvels, the faces and voices of prominent people and so on, than they had before. But fewer than ever have any background for appraising these unrelated, unevaluated, and random bits.[37]

The sanctification of "neutralist" objectivity, against which Wylie writes, has become well established in American journalism. Journalists by and large pay homage to this concept of objectivity, wherein "these unrelated, unevaluated, and random bits" of information comprise objective reporting if they are accurate and verifiable. Of course, many journalists will take issue with this whole line of argument, saying that *any* good reporter avoids presenting "unrelated, unevaluated, and random bits" of information. All I can say is that the journalistic media are filled with news stories which provide superficial bits and pieces of inadequate, meaningless, and useless information. If the reader, viewer, or listener doubts this, he is invited to expose himself in a "focused" way to the news media, especially in regard to a "story" with which he has first-hand knowledge.

Without a doubt the "neutralist perspective" of objectivity dominates today, although the "Fromm-perspective" mentioned above is embraced by existential journalists. This does not mean that existential journalists always *succeed* in their total context reporting, in their "encompassing" journalism; it is a difficult task, and the reporting often falls to the superficial "neutralist" level of shallowness, but at least the existential journalist *tries* for

[36] *The Revolution of Hope* (New York: Bantam Books, 1971), p. 56.
[37] Philip Wylie, *The Magic Animal* (New York: Simon & Schuster—Pocket Books, 1969), p. 205.

something better. He is not content with the one-dimensional "neutralist" concept; he attempts to bring a greater degree of sophistication and honesty into his journalism. He is often frustrated by tradition and by a natural conservatism of plodding and unimaginative editors, but he keeps on trying. And, trying, he inevitably meets with some success even in the most stagnant and reactionary environs.

Action: The Proof of Personhood

The striving of the existential journalist toward a more "encompassing" journalism—a more subjective journalism—is an indication of an action-oriented perspective. On the other hand, the dispassionate, the neutralist, the nonexistential journalist who dominates today's media takes very few actions. At least, he takes few actions of an authentic type; for mainly his activities are routine, expected, predictable, institutionalized ones for which he can take no special credit. He has inserted himself into the giant journalistic computor and has consented in his own mechanistic manipulation. He acts, but his acts are those of the robot who moves this way or that when the proper button is pushed.

Action, I am often told by journalism students and journalists, is dependent on freedom; therefore, if the person has little freedom, he cannot act authentically very often in his journalism. Frequently a student will tell me that he wishes he could do this-or-that on *The Columbia Missourian*.[38] "Have you tried?" I ask. The answer is usually that he has not. He has simply assumed he could not do it; he felt it useless to ask, or to try. In this way, many journalists enslave themselves by their own inaction, their timidity, and reluctance to try anything that departs from the norm. "Keep pushing," I tell the students. "You won't be able to do everything you want to do, but you'll manage to do a lot more than you think you can do." For it has been my observation that a sincere and persistent person can usually get his way—or at least "part" of his way. But most never try, or they give up too soon; and they thereby contribute to the solidification of institutionalized activities and conformity.

---

[38] The University of Missouri School of Journalism's regular, competitive daily newspaper, run as a laboratory paper under the direction of certain faculty members.

Often I have found that, if you believe in something and want to take some action which is in the "twilight zone" of policy, the best course is to go ahead and do it. Often bringing it out in discussion, talking about it, arguing about it, getting it bogged down in institutional red tape, is as good as killing it. So the existential journalist should go ahead and do it, if he thinks it is the proper action to take. Perhaps one time out of ten he will be thwarted in his desired action, or he will have to pay some penalty for having taken it, but in the other nine times he will have succeeded; he will have pushed back the fuzzy limits of restriction; he will have broken new ground; he will have expanded his own world of freedom and the freedom-worlds of others.

It is through these journalistic choices that the existential journalist grows, matures, creates himself, and projects himself into the future. He must choose not simply to desire to act; he must choose to act. His actions prove his personhood.

The very notion of man for the existentialist, according to Macquarrie, turns away from "all static ideas and sees him in action from the first."[39] The emphasis is on man as "an agent," one who insists on action—on doing, not just "being"—for only in action does "existence attain concreteness and fullness."[40] For the existentialist, action does, however, include more than overt activities; it includes both thought and passion. For as Macquarrie says, if thought, passion, and inward decision are lacking, nothing will be left worthy of the name of action. "Thus," Macquarrie adds, "in spite of the premium that the existentialist places upon action, existentialism is not the same as pragmatism."[41] So we can say that action includes more than empirically observable deeds; it includes the thought, the *willing*, the motivations, etc. upon which the observable deeds are based. It is, in a sense, an expression of the *whole* person, and as a person acts, he is "both projecting and realizing an image of personhood."[42]

The non-existential journalist acts, too, as was pointed out earlier, but his acts come from a surface-level of self which is hardly more than a conditioned reflex. These non-existential

---

[39] Macquarrie, *Existentialism*, p. 135.
[40] *Ibid.*, p. 136.
[41] *Ibid.*, p. 137.
[42] *Ibid.*

actions express more about the institution than they do about the person's authentic self. The existential journalist is not a random-actor; he *thinks* before he acts. This "he thinks" is important, for it indicates a motivation to action that transcends a kind of institutional determinism resulting in patterned activities. *He* thinks; *he* wills; *he* acts. His action, in other words, is not a social reflex; rather it is a self-determined action coming from his very being.

Existential action, then, is not random, it is not thoughtless, and it is not simply socially determined. For if it were, it would not be authentic action of the type which would make the person grow, create himself, become.

As Ortega puts it, our actions should not be "random fisticuffs with the things around us or with our fellow men"; for if they are nothing more than this, he says, they have no rationale, no foundation, no serious motivation. "Action," Ortega posits, "is to act upon the environment of material things and on other men in accordance with a plan preconceived in a previous period of meditation or thought."[43] So Ortega insists on thought preceding action; for, as he says, there is "no genuine action if there is no thought, and there is no authentic thought if it is not duly referred to action and made virile by its relation to action."[44] Therefore we can see that thought without action is dead, and action without thought is inauthentic—a kind of subhuman—action.

In conclusion, I should like to make it clear that when I speak of existential journalistic action, I am not referring to emotional and illogical escapades based on passion or instinct. I am talking about predetermined action which the journalist takes on his own, resulting from his own willing. And I am talking about action which the existential journalist thinks is sound and ethical—action which will help reveal his individuality, his personhood, and his concern for himself as a future person-to-be.

---

[43] José Ortega y Gasset, *Man and People* (New York: W. W. Norton & Co., 1963), p. 29.
[44] *Ibid.*

6

In Search of Authenticity

Our own age is essentially one of understanding, and on the average, perhaps, more knowledgeable than any former generation, but it is without passion. Everyone knows a great deal, we all know which way we ought to go and all the different ways we can go, but nobody is willing to move.

—SØREN KIERKEGAARD, *The Present Age*

Let us affront and reprimand the smooth and squalid contentment of the times. . . . a true man belongs to no other time or place, but is the centre of things. . . . I actually am, and do not need for my assurance or the assurance of my fellows any secondary testimony.

—RALPH WALDO EMERSON, *Self-Reliance*

The reality of the world cannot be avoided. Experience of the harshness of the real is the only way by which a man can come to his own self. To play an active part in the world, even though one aims at an impossible goal, is the necessary precondition of one's own being.

—KARL JASPERS, *Man in the Modern Age*

IN THE PRECEDING CHAPTERS a survey has been given of the main aspects of existentialism which apply to what I am calling "existential journalism." All of the characteristics which have been set forth as traits of the existential journalist help to define what may be called *authenticity* in journalism. The existential journalist is ever in the state of becoming authentic. He is, in other words, constantly making himself more honest, more individualistic, more involved and committed, more active, more responsible, and more ethical.

Authenticity: the Elusive Goal

Perhaps the most central quality of authenticity in journalism is a passionate state of mind. As Kierkegaard bemoans the passing of the "passionate age" and the coming of the "reflective age," so also does an existential journalist lament the lack of passion in journalism. To be passionate—to be involved, dedicated, committed to action—is to be truly human; for, as existentialists point out, being born does not assure us that we are human. "On the contrary," says F. H. Heinemann, "it lulls us into pretence."[1] Being human, he adds, is not a fact, but a task; for we are "in constant danger of becoming inhuman."

And, it is very easy to fall to (or never to leave) the level of the "inhuman," for people generally "are inclined to laziness" and they are "timorous," as Nietzsche puts it in his essay on "Schopenhauer as Educator."[2] Men, however, are not as timorous as they are lazy, adds Nietzsche, and "what they fear most is the troubles with which any unconditional honesty and nudity would burden them."[3] To be authentic, to be more than "a factory product," according to Nietzsche, a person "must merely cease being comfortable with himself [and] follow his conscience which shouts at him: 'Be yourself!' "[4]

Existentialism, as we have seen, is basically a philosophy of revolt against mass men, against all of those who have lost their authentic selfhood in modern technological and group-oriented society. All the notable existentialists who have been mentioned earlier—Jaspers, Marcel, Berdyaev, Buber, Ortega, Kierkegaard, Nietzsche, Camus, Sartre, and others—have expressed their deep concern about the inauthentic mode of human existence. To escape from this inauthentic existence a person must fight constantly for true existence; for a person, Ortega states, is not like a stone which "is given its existence." The Spanish philoso-

---

[1] *Existentialism and the Modern Predicament* (London: Adam and Charles Black, 1953), p. 39.
[2] Walter Kaufmann (ed.), *Existentialism from Dostoevsky to Sartre* (New York: New American Library—a Meridian Book, 1975), p. 123.
[3] *Ibid.*
[4] *Ibid.*

pher continues in his *Historia como sistema* (1941): "Man has to be himself in spite of unfavorable circumstances; that means he has to make his own existence at every single moment. He is given the abstract possibility of existing, but not the reality. This he has to conquer hour after hour. Man must earn his life, not only economically but metaphysically."[5] He must, as Nietzsche puts it in *Thus Spake Zarathustra*, "go into the open air, and away from all dusty rooms" in order to be authentic; he must cease being a spectator, "sitting in cool shade."[6]

A person must constantly pledge himself to the future; he must "engage himself," and as Kierkegaard has described it in *Either/Or*, he must make some kind of "leap" beyond the immediate situation so that he commits himself to circumstances which have not yet become clear. For the existentialist, traditional and routine ways of doing things are anathema since they are not on a truly human level; there is no engagement, no commitment, and no real choice. Therefore, on such an inauthentic level, the journalist would be merely acting as an automaton and not as a real, existing person. It is through this choosing, this commitment, this willed action—as we have seen—that a person develops character and an authentic self. He chooses, he acts, and he accepts responsibility. As Koestenbaum says, "existentialism holds man fully responsible for his actions and inactions; it does not displace blame onto upbringing, heredity, and environment."[7] So, not only the willing, the choosing, and the action contribute to the journalist's authenticity, but also the accepting of personal responsibility for the action.

There seem to be two main orientations among existentialists: (1) concern with changing *directly* the outer conditions of men's lives—a kind of "external" rebellion, exemplified by Sartre, and (2) concern with altering society *indirectly* through changes man can effect in himself, exemplified by Camus. Germaine Brée has called these existential emphases the "Promethean" (Sartre) and the "Orphic" (Camus).[8] The Prome-

---

[5] Quoted in *Ibid.*, pp. 153-54.

[6] Quoted in Brian V. Hill, *Education and the Endangered Individual: A Critique of Ten Modern Thinkers* (New York: Dell Publishing Co.—a Laurel Edition, 1973), p. 56.

[7] Peter Koestenbaum, *Philosophy: A General Introduction* (New York: American Book Co., 1968), p. 322.

[8] *Camus and Sartre* (New York: Dell Publishing Co.—Delta Books, 1972), pp. 240-45 *passim*.

thean tradition in journalism stresses defying the established powers frontally, directly; the Promethean journalist is, as Sartre has put it, the extrinsic rebel. The Orphic tradition, on the other hand, stresses a transformation from within; it is more internal, passive, and concerned more with the Self than social reform.[9] Prometheanism, in effect, seeks to change the outer conditions of men's lives, whereas Orphism seeks to alter society indirectly through changes a person can bring about in himself.[10]

Brée, in *Camus and Sartre*, says that Sartre set two main goals for the journalist and writer: (1) to unveil, disclose to his readers the developing patterns of the social world, and to disclose and judge social weaknesses, and (2) to join action personally to thought, to close the gap between knowledge and practice.[11] For Camus, the task of a journalist is mainly concerned "with the present, with the practical needs of the moment" for, according to Brée, he was "not trying either to detect or to regulate the current of history." Camus's confrontations are mainly with himself; he may have to struggle against others, but he does not "judge" them.[12] In the opinion of Camus, each man is his own Sisyphus; this contrasts with Sartre's sense that his task is "the role of guide and teacher"—to force people to see their lives in clear intellectual perspective.[13]

Even though each existential journalist may be inclined toward Prometheanism or toward Orphism, if he is a true existentialist he will be concerned with both orientations. He will want to improve his society (fighting against inauthentic elements outside himself) and he will also be committed to improving himself (struggling against inauthentic inclinations within himself).

Authenticity in Journalism Education

Journalism educators have an important role to play in respect to the development of authenticity and to existential journalism generally. They can help to provide an environment where existentialism thrives, or they can create an atmosphere

---

[9] *Ibid.*, pp. 252-53.
[10] *Ibid.*, p. 253.
[11] *Ibid.*, p. 241.
[12] *Ibid.*, p. 240.
[13] *Ibid.*

destructive to such an environment. Usually, I believe, they participate in the latter enterprise, and there are several reasons for their non-existential stance.

First off, they themselves are "corporate" people, institutionalized functionaries, and escapists from freedom. They have come from newsrooms where they have been efficiently depersonalized, or they have spent most of their working lives in Academe where, in spite of many myths about academic freedom and the healthy toleration of eccentric and deviant viewpoints, hierarchical pressures and political game-playing have gone far in depersonalizing and frightening the professor. In either case, the average journalism professor is an "expediency expert," shedding his integrity and basic honesty for an assurance of flexible working hours, frequent vacations, regular promotions, tenure, and salary increases that are not related to what he actually does.[14] Both campus and newsroom very effectively serve as breeding spots for non-existential journalists.

In the newsroom, for example, each staff member finds himself in a well-defined little niche, having little freedom to use his individuality and creativity except in highly proscribed ways in very narrow confines. He may often think of himself as having considerable freedom, but really he has become ever more institutionalized and imbued with the "corporate mentality." Deep down, perhaps, he really knows that he has little real freedom—that he suffers far more from "manipulation" and "direction" from his superiors than his medium suffers from Government or other "outside" entities. He has come to think of journalistic freedom as meaning only freedom of the press (as an institution) from outside forces; he seldom permits himself to think about journalistic freedom *as it relates to him as he works within journalism itself.*

But, after all, this is the system. And after all, journalism *is* private enterprise; the media (at least the print media) are owned by individuals and are in the private sector. So it is only natural that the "boss" is in charge of his employees, that the publishers and editors, directors and managers, exercise control over their

---

[14] Certainly there are some notable exceptions to this general timidity among journalism professors. Some of the most intellectually active and courageous teachers I have known have been in journalism. Every journalism student could, I'm sure, name at least one such journalism teacher. These exceptional teachers, however, are certainly a small minority, not only in journalism departments, but anywhere on the campus today.

enterprises. Therefore, the force of capitalistic theory combined with the traditional employer-employee relationship tends to ingrain deeply (and early) a sense of individual impotence in journalists; by and large they are educated to accept a kind of subservience and timidity, a kind of corporation-mentality which permits them to step into the world of journalism with a feeling of security and stability. They are educated to be harmonious zombies, and generally, that is exactly what they are.

Journalism education must bear a large part of the responsibility for this state of affairs. For journalism education, however hard it may try to avoid it, is a force projecting students toward a kind of "vocationalism," replete with conservative tendencies. The emphasis is on functionalism, on technique, on conformity to basic objectives. As Fred Hechinger says in a provocative article in *Saturday Review*, this "new vocationalism" sweeping American campuses emphasizes careerism, with a natural tendency to screen out students who do not seem to fit some standard prescribed by a vocational elite. It is marked, says Hechinger, by conservatives (e.g., Gerald Ford's "new realism") and by a drift toward specialization.[15]

A kind of "indoctrination" has replaced "liberal education" as a goal in most journalism schools and departments. Concern with the "right ways to do things" is replacing a lively regard for experimentation, free-ranging intellectual curiosity, and a concern for and questioning of, established doctrine. Learn the doctrine and accept it; don't challenge it: this is the core of modern journalism educational theory. Increasingly, technique consumes the academic life of journalism students; it is true that this concern with technique is taking computerized and other technological directions, but it is still *technical* in nature.

More and more journalism programs in colleges and universities are increasing their "core" courses, leaving fewer and fewer "electives" for the students. At the same time journalism programs are eliminating basic course requirements in psychology, sociology, and philosophy, which once played a large part in journalism education. Foreign languages are going by the board—and this at a time when educators pay lip service to cosmopolitanism in all its aspects. English courses, once strong in the university education of a person going into journalism,

---

[15] Fred M. Hechinger, "Murder in Academe: The Demise of Education," *Saturday Review* (March 20, 1976), pp. 11-18.

play little part today in the journalism student's curriculum. But, the journalism student gets hundreds of hours of training in writing leads, headlines, advertising copy, reading news before a camera, and on and on. Strangely, however, he gets little or no theory and practice in interviewing—probably the most important "technique" which a journalist can have. This is perhaps because interviewing, unlike writing headlines or pasting up a newspaper page, is a "humanistic," rather than a routine technique.

To give maximum opportunity for the development of existential journalism, journalism education programs would have to change drastically; at present they are drifting toward more and more "professionalism"—toward more concern with mechanisms, methods, forms, and techniques. They are attempting to standardize journalism more and more, not to diversify it. They are concerned with giving students the "right" and "pragmatic" (traditional) methods so they can step easily into the "professional" world of journalism. Conformity has set in—even in so-called research courses, which often push a certain methodology to the virtual exclusion of others. Courses teach how to do this or that, how to conform to prevailing practices. Seldom are these practices challenged or questioned; seldom are experiments undertaken to see if new ways will work better or just as well.[16] What is emphasized is *not* the creativity of the student. This is too often stifled. Even when certain professors do permit some creativity, it must be well within the accepted limits of safe and acceptable deviation.

In my more than a quarter century of teaching journalism, I have seen the spark of creativity killed many times. Bright, ambitious, eager, excited, expectant students have come into journalism programs only to be discouraged again and again. They have largely been molded into uncritical conformists, beaten into shape by machine-like curricula and machine-like teachers, and by strict requirements of a lock-step program which gives each student a minimum chance for individual development. Certainly, the program which would best create existential

---

[16] When a journalism program does try to experiment and change traditional educational practices, as the University of Iowa School of Journalism did a few years back under the leadership of the late Dr. Malcolm MacLean, "professional journalists" and accrediting groups for journalism education manage to put enough pressure on the experimenters so that they are soon back in the traditional mold.

journalists would be as open and flexible as possible, offering the student the greatest chance to pursue his own special interests, to go in his own direction, with the least possible stereotyping. This is not the same as endorsing "permissiveness" (which signifies a non-concern for the student's future), and it is not a denial that the student cannot learn from teachers or that he knows best in all cases what he needs.

Perhaps one reason journalism students are not often intellectually stimulated is that their professors themselves are not intellectually oriented. Very often journalism teachers are shallow and superficial; often, too, they are dull and unenthusiastic. Of course, this can be said of teachers in any academic field, but myriads of students can attest to the general intellectual slovenliness and the lack of a catalytic quality in journalism faculty members. Unfortunately, too many of them are in need of an education themselves. Great numbers of them are jaded practitioners who have "retired" to Academe (and the number is growing rapidly); they run out of personal anecdotes very soon and have to think up "busy work" to pass the hours in the classroom, turning over more and more duties to student assistants. They seldom read; they are seldom seen in the university libraries; they seldom think and discuss issues and problems in journalism with colleagues—especially those in other departments. They retire into their own little worlds, reveling in the memory of the "good old days" when they were out there practicing journalism. They have very few new ideas because they don't think about vital problems very often. They don't dare encourage students to experiment and think creatively. Why? Because they don't do it themselves; it is small wonder that "lock-step" teaching is the rule, rather than the exception, in journalism schools and departments.

The concept of authenticity relates to journalism teachers as well as to practicing journalists. And one of the principal aspects of authenticity is integrity—a kind of basic honesty which manifests itself in the person's being himself, saying what he thinks, acting only in such ways that are consistent with his own ethical standards. Erich Fromm, who has been quoted often in these pages, has said that respect for one's own integrity and uniqueness is inseparable from respect for and understanding of other individuals.[17]

17 *Man for Himself*, pp. 133-34.

When the journalism educator has respect for himself, he will teach existentially and will generally expand the existential horizons of his school or department. He will enthrone not only his own individuality, but the individuality of his students. He will insist on personalism, not impersonalism; he will encourage diversity in his students, not conformity; he will try to give free reign to creativity, not imitation. He will constantly attempt to get the students into "deep waters," encourage them to take chances, make choices, accept responsibilities. The existential teacher abides by Kierkegaard's advice to call to those younger than himself to jump into the waves—to "leap cheerfully, even if it means a lighthearted leap, so long as it is decisive."[18] Far too many who are swimming today, as Kierkegaard notes, are doing it in shallow waters. What the existential journalism teacher will try to do is to get the student out of these "shallow waters" of mechanistic thinking and acting into the deeper waters of intellectual concern where giant waves buffet them around.

What the existential journalism professor says is that the very base of journalism education should be intellectual liberation. Where this assumption does not exist, where education is understood in purely technical or professional terms, it would be better to eliminate journalism from the curriculum. What Peter Berger says so well of sociology can also be said of journalism as an academic course of study: "Sociology is justified by the belief that it is better to be conscious than unconscious and that consciousness is a condition of freedom. To attain a greater measure of awareness, and with it of freedom, entails a certain amount of suffering and even risk. An educational process that would avoid this becomes simple technical training and ceases to have any relationship to the civilizing of the mind."[19] If we in journalism education do not heed Berger's words and stress liberal education, creative thought and action, and intellectual freedom, we will join forces with other social pressures depersonalizing education and indoctrinating for conformity.

The concept of "professionalism" is very popular today in journalism education. On all sides I hear references to "professional schools of journalism." I hear talk of the student becoming

---

[18] Søren Kierkegaard, *The Present Age* (New York: Harper Torchbooks, 1962), pp. 26-37 *passim*.

[19] Peter L. Berger, *Invitation to Sociology: A Humanistic Perspective* (Garden City, N.Y.: Doubleday Anchor Books, 1963), p. 175.

a "professional." I hear about "professionalism" in journalism constantly, but I seldom hear a meaning given to it. One thing is certain: use of the term indicates a kind of growing elitism, a kind of exclusiveness, a kind of "special" in-group thinking which is growing in journalism education and in journalism itself. Specialization is probably at the root of this trend; as William Barrett says, "Specialization is the price we pay for the advancement of knowledge." He adds that it is "a price" because the "path of specialization leads away from the ordinary and concrete acts of understanding in terms of which man actually lives his day-to-day life."[20]

As journalism becomes more and more specialized, it is perhaps only natural that it would seek a "professional status" like medicine and law. There seems to be a natural desire to be "exclusive," to be prestigious, and the term "professional" seems to connote something with these "elitist" overtones. When someone says to me: "We have a professional school of journalism," I immediately wonder which schools of journalism are *not* professional. If they are all professional, then, of course, there would be no need to call any of them professional. So far as I know, they all attempt to accomplish the same goal—basically to prepare students to practice journalism. So, perhaps they are all professional, although I base my hope for the future of dynamic and existential journalism on the belief that at least some of them will be *non*-professional.

For it is my contention that journalism (in spite of pronouncements and ethical codes of "professional" societies like Sigma Delta Chi) is not a profession at all and that it should not be one. No existential journalist would want to be a part of a "profession." This would tend to suppress his authentic self, to bind him with rules and procedures, to insist that he meet minimal "entrance" requirements, that he be licensed, that he be given a code to follow or a creed to swear allegiance to—all of which would depersonalize him, make him a conformist, and give him little play to his will. The existentialist wants no part of it. He wants no part of a "profession" where some elite will be saying what journalists should or should not do, what their duties and responsibilities should be, etc. In fact, such professionalization would take away the pluralism and freedom such as still

---

[20] William Barrett, *Irrational Man*, p.7.

exist in America. The existential journalist sees this, and rebels against it. He wants as few strictures on his freedom as possible. He sees himself as his *own* profession, and he is committed to his own "professional" standards—and to no one else's.

The existential journalist considers consequences for printing this or that. He must make decisions as to what, how much of, and in what way, to print. In making these decisions, he makes himself as a journalist. He thrusts himself into the world, and lives harmoniously with his subjectivity. Many standard or Establishment *status-quo* (non-existential) journalists say that professionalism demands this or that. Why? Whose professionalism? Where does such a definition of professionalism—or of journalism in a free society, for that matter—come from? The only real duty of an existential journalist is to be free, and to take upon himself the responsibility for his freedom. And it is really to himself that he has this responsibility—to his existential self, to his values, insights, beliefs, commitments. It is thus that he becomes truly authentic, a *real* journalist, not a puppet-journalist, one moving to the cadence of the group or the dictates of the editor or publisher.

Making as many personal decisions as possible, the existential journalist exercises his freedom; he exercises his editorial prerogative to the maximum, just as the editor does. In fact, the existential reporter *is* an editor. He determines what will be news and what kind of news it will be; he fashions it, makes it, subjugates it to his will. He makes the world in his own image—and, in reality, makes the world for his audience. He subjectivizes constantly, and cannot escape it; his newsstories cannot transcend himself; they are subjective simply because he is the reporting *subject.* He must recognize this, assert it, confirm it—and certainly he should not apologize for it. Why should he try to blot himself out by affirming neutralism and "objectivity"?

Standard journalism deemphasizes the journalist and emphasizes the reportorial object or the "issue" under discussion. Existential journalism emphasizes the journalist; it is *through* him, not *by* him, that we get a glimpse of the world beyond our direct and immediate perception. The existential journalist's perceptions, sensitivities, judgments, evaluations, and the like, *are part of* the reality of the situation and should not be sublimated in the name of objectivity. Standard journalism distorts through stressing objectivity—which is really a sort of pseudo-journalism, depersonalized and mechanistic to the point of confusing fact with reality, accuracy with truth. The existential journalist knows better; he knows he is a *subject* and not an object, and that he as a reporter must, therefore, be subjective. Subjectivity is valued and used, not apologized for.

Returning to journalism education, it should be noted that very little of the existential perspectives noted above have deep roots (or any roots at all) in the Journalistic Mills of Academe. Very few professors are existentialists. Fewer administrators are existentialists. And, for many, many persons—probably for the vast majority of those who read these words—this is a fortunate situation; for an existentialist emphasis is likely seen as a great danger to smooth-running academic productivity. Would not existentialism, many ask, make inoperative a sound philosophy of education—which, by its very nature, implies considerable conformity and indoctrination?

But, actually, there is no real need for academic administrators or their bosses on boards and in legislatures to worry too much about the rise of journalistic existentialism. And there is no need for the publishers of newspapers and magazines, the directors of broadcasting stations, to become anxious about their loss of power in the face of an existential revolution in their media: for the existential journalist is not good at organizing—in fact, he rebels against it—and the individualistic existentialist is hardly to be considered a potent force against the giant institutionalized power bureaucracy of the American mass media or the American university. The existential journalist and journalism educator will fight; they will struggle; they will do their bit against the "system" here and there, but they will not make substantial changes in the ever-enlarging conformity which is encircling us all.

Ethics and Authenticity

It is difficult to discuss ethics from the existential perspective. This is because of the very personal, *self*-deterministic nature of existentialism. And generally the subject of ethics carries with it a *social*-deterministic emphasis. We often assume that an ethics is formulated and enforced by some group of peers or by society at large. For example, we speak of legal ethics, or medical ethics, or social ethics. And, therefore, it is natural that those in journalism think about "journalistic ethics," implying some normative rules or standards to which *those in journalism* are somehow bound. This is a concept of ethics which, in a sense, binds the journalist to the norms of *the group*, leads him into a kind of conformist posture. And, what is more, in most cases the journalist has little or nothing to do with the formulation of the ethical code that bears on him. Little wonder the existential journalist has little faith in, or obligation to, codes of ethics.

Let us look briefly at one such journalistic code. In 1973 the Society of Professional Journalists, Sigma Delta Chi, adopted a "Code of Ethics." It, like most ethical codes, is an organizational code, filled with generalizations and semantically foggy clichés. Such phrases stating that SDX'ers believe in "public enlightenment as the forerunner of justice," "obligations that require journalists to perform with intelligence, objectivity, accuracy, and fairness," and serving "the general welfare" are to be found.

The Code enthrones "responsibility" and declares that journalists "who use their professional status as representatives of the public for selfish or other unworthy motives violate a high trust." Existential journalists will be surprised to hear that SDX considers them as having "professional status" or that selfish motives are naturally "unworthy." Then, the Code proceeds to state such vague glittering generalities as that "journalists uphold the right to speak unpopular opinions and the privilege to agree with the majority." One interesting statement in the Code is that journalists "must be free of obligation to any interest other than the public's right to know the truth." If that is really the case, then why does SDX come out with a Code of Ethics, in which it attempts to place many *other* obligations on the journalists?

The SDX Code runs through the usual litany of "don'ts"— such as not taking gifts, free trips, special treatment, and secondary employment. We are even told that journalists should refrain from "political involvement, holding office, and service in community organizations"; such activities are all right, of course, if they do not compromise "the integrity of journalists and their employers." Then, the Code tells SDX members that "so-called news communications from private sources should not be published or broadcast without substantiation of their claims to news value." This is indeed a strange statement. Does it mean that if the journalist "substantiates" that a private source *claims* the item has "news value," then it should be published? That is exactly what it says. Whether or not the item is true, or in fact *does* have news value, seems to matter not at all. Also, one might wonder about "news communications" from *public* sources, as well as "private sources"; would SDX'ers not want to check them out?

On and on goes the Code, setting up guidelines for the organization-persons. Truth is mentioned as the ultimate goal; then objectivity in reporting is set up as another goal, although it would seem this is tautological. The SDX'er is told that "there is no excuse for inaccuracies or lack of thoroughness," although he knows, if he manages to think at all for himself, that there are *plenty* of excuses for inaccuracies and that "lack of thoroughness" is so vague as to be meaningless. He knows that *no* report is thorough; it is all a matter of degree, and SDX, unfortunately, does not tell the journalist how much thoroughness is enough.

Then we are told by the Code that "news reports should be free of opinion or bias and represent all sides of an issue." This is a fascinating statement in its lack of realism or achievability. It is impossible to keep news reports free of opinion, and SDX journalists fill their stories every day with opinion of one kind or another—if not their own, then somebody else's. And, as to representing "all sides of an issue," any thoughtful reporter knows that there are any number of sides to issues (this is why they are issues), and that it is impossible to represent in any news report *all* sides of any issue. Journalists cannot even represent *all issues*, much less all sides of issues.

The Code goes into matters of "fair play," and states that journalists will respect "the dignity, rights and well-being of people encountered in the course of gathering and presenting the news," will "guard against invading a person's right to privacy," will not "pander to morbid curiosity about details of vice and crime," and will make prompt and complete correction of errors, and what is probably most interesting—that journalists will "be accountable to the public for their reports." Just what does this last "accountability" clause mean? How will journalists be accountable? This is the kind of language in journalistic codes which render them generally meaningless, or, at least, suspect.

Then, at the very end of the Code of Ethics, there is a "pledge." It reads as follows:

Journalists should actively censure and try to prevent violations

of these standards, and they should encourage their observance
by all newspeople. Adherence to this code of ethics is intended to
preserve the bond of mutual trust and respect between American
journalists and the American people.

Fair enough. But one thing is certain: the "bond of mutual trust"
might be preserved (if it is there) between journalists and
non-journalists in our society, but what about "mutual trust"
among journalists themselves? It is easy to imagine what would
happen if journalists took the "pledge" seriously and began
"actively" censuring their colleagues and trying to prevent
violations of this fuzzy and generalized Code of Ethics. Also the
thought occurs: If there is mutual trust and respect between
American journalists and the American people, how did it
develop without the Code of Ethics which SDX feels must
preserve it?

The real point of bringing up this Code here is to show that
really it is nothing more than high-sounding rhetoric; it may be
worthy of framing and hanging on the wall, but that is all. It
pretends to be "public" or "group" in its orientation—having a
kind of binding effect on SDX journalists—but it really is not a
legitimate code for this very reason. It can be nothing but
personal—as the individual interprets it—at its best; but when it
becomes "personal," it loses its reason for being. Why not simply
let the individual journalist frame his *own code* in his own words,
internally, and change it from time to time in his own time and in
his own way? The only valid ethics is that which is within each
person. The existential journalist knows this very well, and this
is why he cannot take seriously any normative ethical code,
however beautifully produced it may be.

*   *   *

Existentialism, by and large, is not very clear on the matter of
ethics; this is due, as was said earlier, to its personal nature.
Intrinsic in existentialism is the rebellion against firm rules and
collectivized standards. The *person* is enthroned, not the group.
As ethics comes into play in existentialism at all, it is an
individualistic ethics, a very personal thing. It leaves many
specific questions unanswered; in this sense, it cannot be forced
into the straightjacket of a "code." Hazel Barnes, in a book on
existentialist ethics, says, "The perfectly coherent, rigidly ob-

served code of ethics may well be maintained at the cost of foregoing all spontaneity."[21] She continues: "To be perfectly what one has chosen to be will inevitably exclude much that is precious in what he might otherwise have been."[22]

To some extent, the "pure" existentialist might say that the non-ethical choice is as good as the ethical choice—since both are authentic. But a good case can be made for choosing to be ethical. Hazel Barnes deals with this in these words:

> In insisting that one ought to choose to be ethical, we are on sure ground in affirming at least these things: First, the choice not to be ethical is almost wholly a rejection. Its bare minimum of positive value is the true recognition that one is in fact free not to subject himself to any demands whatsoever if he so chooses. . . . The purely nonethical life is as impossible to sustain practically as the perfectly ethical one. Insofar as it can be lived, it takes the form of rejecting all rational calculation, all responsibility for others and for one's own past and future—at least in the sense of feeling that one's acts should be governed by such con- siderations. It places all value on spontaneous self-realization and none on the temporal kind. Thus it is a choice of subjectivity and a rejection of objectivity, not an expansion of life but a reduc- tion.[23]

So really, what we can say is that if a person chooses to be nonethical, he is choosing not-to-be or not-becoming; he is choosing Nothingness, and this is contrary to the ideals of the existentialist. The existentialist will choose to be ethical. And, as most existentialists say, rationality must be introduced as one of the criteria even though, as Barnes puts it, "it may at the same time insist that its goal is happiness or satisfaction or some other state which is closer to emotion than to reason."[24]

The importance of ethics to the existentialist is the degree to which we *act* ethically; a person may have all kinds of personal values—even down on paper (e.g., a Code of Ethics)—but one's actual life goes on as if the ethical did not exist. Existentialists— especially those taking their ethical cues from Kierkegaard— believe that the fundamental choice is not the choice between rival concepts of good and bad, but the "choice by which we

---

[21] Hazel E. Barnes, *An Existentialist Ethics* (New York: Random House Vintage Books, 1967), p. 21.

[22] *Ibid.*, p. 22.

[23] *Ibid.*, pp. 23-25 *passim*.

[24] *Ibid.*, p. 26.

summon good and bad into existence for ourselves."[25] Without such a choice, William Barrett says, an abstract system of ethics is just so "much paper currency with nothing to back it up."[26]

An individual can break with the ethical, "but he must have subordinated himself to the ethical universal; and the break, when he is called upon to make it, is made in fear and trembling and not in the callous arrogance of power," according to Barrett.[27] And the grounds for breaking with the ethical (in the sense of a kind of "social ethics"), to Kierkegaard, is the basic principle "that the individual is higher than the universal." As Barrett adds, "The universal rule of ethics, precisely because it is universal, cannot comprehend totally me, the individual, in my concreteness."[28] When something goes against a person's deepest self, then he is compelled to break (or transcend) the generally accepted ethics of his society; when one follows conscience he rises above ethics. "I am compelled to make an exception because I myself *am* an exception; that is, a concrete being whose existence can never be completely subsumed under any universal or even system of universals," Barrett writes.[29] This "suspension of the ethical" is illustrated poignantly in Kierkegaard's story of Abraham and Isaac in *Fear and Trembling*.

Ethics must be personal if it is to contribute to the authenticity of the journalist. Following some group-designed code or traditional manner of action, either out of blind submission or thoughtless habit, is inauthentic and depersonalizing. Existentialism has often been criticized as a philosophical support for a kind of anarchical position in ethics; this, however, is unfair, for most conceptions of existentialism neither scorn rationality nor see the individual as detached from other individuals. In fact, in several existentialists (especially Sartre) there is a kind of Kantianism to be found: when the person chooses, they say, he is choosing not only for himself but for everybody. A similarity to Kant's Categorical Imperative can be noted here.

The basic point is this: no real blueprint exists for what the individual journalist can become, or what he should do. He must decide for himself. Each journalist's existence is his own. There is no universal pattern of journalism that can be imposed upon

---

[25] *Irrational Man*, p. 165.
[26] *Ibid.*
[27] *Ibid.*, p. 167.
[28] *Ibid.*
[29] *Ibid.*

him, to which he must conform. He must impose his own pattern on himself; but, more, he must constantly realize that this pattern will change—should change—and that his "demands upon himself" will be dynamic, not static.

A journalist becomes authentic, becomes truly himself, only to the extent that he freely chooses himself. His existence is authentic to the degree that he guides himself—or to the degree he has molded himself in his own individual image. The inauthentic journalist, on the contrary, is molded largely by external influences: circumstances, ethical codes, professional standards, habit, media authorities, or whatever. Of course, every journalist *must* be molded to some degree by outside forces; this is unavoidable. But the point here is that he *maximize* his own formation or molding and that he determine that these "depersonalizing" forces be held at arm's length. And this is a constant, full-time job, for the natural tendency is for him to conform, to slip into easy routine, and slowly lose personal authenticity.

But, many readers will ask, is not this orientation dangerous and unrealistic? Does it not lead to a complete relativism—even anarchy? In such a situation, how could morality have any real meaning for society? Are we going to end up with a kind of "chaos" in which every journalist "does his own thing"?

These questions suggest an unwarranted assumption about existentialism. No major existentialist philosopher has ever suggested that everything is permitted. Always there is some control. A kind of reasonableness, for instance, which will keep personal freedom in bounds, is quite common in existentialist literature. Or Christian "love," as in Kierkegaard's case, where a real concern for others keeps personal freedom under control. Or, as it is with Sartre, the control is exercised by his notion of responsibility. For as he sees it, the anguish of a choice arises from the fact that, in making the choice, a person is committing not only himself but, in a certain manner, all mankind. This, as has been suggested, is almost Kantian: one chooses then only those things which he would be willing to see universalized. This certainly keeps a rational person from going too far in "doing his own thing." Also—and this is important: the existential journalist *never* tries to escape the consequences for his authenticity, for his freely determined actions. There are always his superiors. He can always be fired. He must understand this; *he* alone must decide whether or not to take the risk.

Another Kantian concept creeps into existentialism. Camus

brings it up when he insists that every person must refuse to be treated as an object (*The Rebel*). To be treated as an object—or to treat others as objects—is an inauthentic situation, completely depersonalizing. Camus is implying that *all* is not permitted, and that the existential journalist, for example, must exercise controls on himself and must feel responsibility to others and a concern for others. The existentialist is not against controls; he simply rebels against these controls coming from *outside* agents.

Another check on the use of freedom is what Luka Brajnovic, a Yugoslav philosopher now teaching in Spain, calls "human dignity." He contends that this dignity places just limits on freedom for the simple reason that man does not live isolated in society; all members have this same human dignity.[30] And this human dignity he refers to, just what is it? We are told that the "moral man" has it. And who is this moral man? The man who does not succumb to his instincts or to his passions; who does not change his opinion without justification; is not a flatterer or renegade. Brajnovic calls all of these characteristics "monstrosities" which negate dignity, as well as the rights and the liberty of man.[31]

A person is also controlled by "conscience," however vague this concept may be. It may mean a person's awareness of the moral code accepted in his society, together with the feelings of discomfort or satisfaction that he may have as he either breaks or keeps the code. But it is also the term used for the kind of moral conviction that will sometimes lead a person to reject the accepted standards of his society in response to what he believes to be a more deeply rooted imperative. Existentialists tend to find more meaning in the second of these two senses; as has been mentioned earlier, Kierkegaard deals with "conscience" in this second sense in his *Fear and Trembling*. Nietzsche even goes further than Kierkegaard; he not only would suspend conventional moral obligations on occasion, but would transcend them completely. For him, the commonly accepted morality is like the "old broken tables" of the law; Nietzsche's concern is for the "Superman" who will go beyond man as he is.[32]

Heidegger seems to think of a "deeper conscience" that

---

[30] Luka Brajnovic, *Deontología Periodística* (Pamplona: Ediciones Universidad de Navarra, S.A., 1969), p. 151.

[31] *Ibid.*, p. 224.

[32] Macquarrie, *Existentialism*, p. 166.

delivers us from a kind of "public" conscience—from the moral dictates of "they." For Heidegger, true conscience summons the true self (*Dasein*) from its lostness in the "they." Only when the person stops listening to the voice of "they" can he truly hear the call of conscience, and become truly authentic. The source of this call? Heidegger suggests that it comes from the very depth of one's own being. It is the struggle of the authentic self to be born. And the "content" of the call? There is no content; it varies with the person, for each must seek to realize his own potentiality for being.[33]

In order to be more existential and more authentic, the journalist will promote in himself the basic Nietzschean theme of saying "yes to life" thereby becoming more noble and heroic— and thus more authentic.[34] The existential journalist would be something of a Nietzschean Superman—a person who has learned to transcend himself, to rise to his highest potential. He would be a "higher man"—a kind of law unto himself, a center of virtue, and a powerful, happy person of exuberant self-expression and self-confidence.[35] A key concept of Nietzsche, consistent with his existentialist orientation, is his passionate belief in the worth of the individual and his view of the hero as the person who does not submit to authority—or at least fights constantly against it.[36]

*   *   *

In conclusion, the point should be reemphasized that authenticity for the existential journalist comes from within; it rises up from the deep wells of the existent himself (*Dasein*) and it exhibits itself through actions which are taken deliberately and based on the absolute integrity of the journalist. Journalism educators and practicing journalists find themselves often living on inauthentic levels; on these levels they are evading choices and actions, they are speaking hypocritical words, they are

---

[33] *Ibid.*

[34] Karl Jaspers, *Nietzsche: An Introduction to the Understanding of His Philosophical Activity* (Chicago: Henry Regnery Co.—a Gateway Edition, 1969), p. 167 ff.

[35] See E. L. Allen, "The Superman" (Ch. 5) in *From Plato to Nietzsche* (Greenwich, Conn.: Fawcett Publications—a Premier Book, 1964), pp. 180-82.

[36] Bertrand Russell, *The Will to Doubt* (New York: Philosophical Library—the Wisdom Library, 1958), p. 101.

retreating from their own freedom, and they are refusing to make for themselves real existence.

In addition, they have refused to take responsibility for their own actions—or inactions, often shifting the blame to someone else. Too often, also, they have turned away from respect for themselves and have hidden in organizations, groups, societies and the like which seem to give them psychological relief from the anxieties and pain of authentic living. These teachers and journalists would be wise to heed the words of St. Augustine who wrote: "*Noli foras ire, in te redi, in interiore homine veritas habitat*"—"Do not desire to go out; return into yourself; truth lives within the inner man."[37]

---

[37] Edmund Husserl, *Cartesian Meditations*, trans. D. Cairns (The Hague: Nijhoff, 1960), p. 157.

7

Postscript: *Carpe Diem*

EXISTENTIAL JOURNALISM, as we have seen, is action-oriented. Through acting, and through being willing to take responsibility for such action, the journalist creates a *self*. This self-creation is a daily thing; it never ends and it is manifested in the journalist's reaching to the past for helpful guiding principles for living and looking to the future for worthwhile objectives. But what is paramount for the existential journalist is *today*—or, better, this very minute. The existential journalist's imperative is this: acting now, committing one's self now, and not waiting for some more suitable or appropriate time for taking a stand in the world.

Carpe diem, the Roman insistence that one "seize the day" or take the present opportunity, is the watchword of the existential journalist. Push out, involve self, take chances, have faith, love the excitement of living and coming in contact with new experiences, people, and cultures. No sitting passively in safe corners for the existential journalist; no doing the same old things in the same old ways; no conversing with the same people; and no drawing away from potentially dangerous situations.

Existential journalists in the 1990s are as hard to find as they were in the 1970s. Maybe even harder. This is probably due to the increasing group-mindedness or collective consciousness that has increased due to many factors, among them exploding populations, an increased reliance on government, a sensed need for group solidarity, and an increasing antipathy to individual isolation.

The Challenge of Communitarianism

A kind of war seems to be heating up (again) between advocates of social journalistic practices of group-involvement (communitarianism) and the individualism and libertarianism of eighteenth-century Enlightenment liberalism. For a long time this was nothing more than a cold war in which proponents of some kind of collectivism or groupism stressed the importance of social interaction and concern, while tolerating those who placed emphasis on the individual, personal development, and maximum autonomy. The two ideological camps were able to coexist rather amicably—at least in the United States.

Today, however, in the fractured society with its rising sense of tribalism, nationalism, and culturalism leading to explosive activities that endanger social cohesion and stability, the old ideological cold war between the *social* or *communitarian* journalists and the *individual* or *libertarian* journalists has worsened. Quite naturally, existential journalists find themselves mainly in the latter camp, stressing as they do personal decision-making and maximum autonomy.

This cleavage between the two journalistic worldviews is really nothing new. It stems from ancient Greece, with Plato espousing a kind of collectivist or social philosophy and Aristotle stressing the development of the individual person. We see these main emphases appearing throughout history—collectivistic social thinkers, such as Rousseau, Hegel, and Marx urging people to consider society more important than their own selves, and individualistic libertarian thinkers, such as Locke, Mill, Voltaire, and Constant, enthroning self-determination and personal freedom.

Adding their voices to the libertarian chorus of the Enlightenment philosophers were the early freedom-loving existentialists, such as Kierkegaard and Nietzsche, and their twentieth-century successors—people such as Sartre, Camus, Buber, Heidegger, and Jaspers. Of course, the cleavage between the two ideologies has never been simple. In the eighteenth-century British and French Enlightenment, for example, there was a certain degree of ambivalence among proponents of individual freedom and those championing social demands. There was a streak of individualism in the statist and a streak of statism or socialism in the individualist-libertarian. John Stuart Mill, in nineteenth-century England, is a good example. Although he was a firm believer in individual freedom, he was a utilitarian who believed in benefits (happiness) that should accrue to the society—to the majority of the people. And Karl Marx, seeing the social benefits as outweighing personal or individual desires and concerns, was ultimately envisioning a more contented, happier, more fulfilled individual person.

Although I have placed the emphasis in this book on the individual and individual freedom, I have not intended to impugn the importance of social interaction. No Enlightenment liberal would have done that; nor would any of the existentialists. Obviously there has to be a mutualism in journalism: *There must be a concern both for the individual and for the social fabric in which the individual functions.*

Individualism Under Siege

The communitarian spirit has made significant inroads into the older and more individualistic realm where the spirit of the European Enlightenment has dominated for so long. A dwindling number of classical liberals and existentialists raise their voices against this tidal wave of collective-action philosophy. For instance, the German existentialists Martin Heidegger and Friedrich Nietzsche have warned of the encroachment of "groupism" and the concomitant disappearance of individualism. And scattered voices today are re-issuing this warning. Heidegger argued against collective social identity in terms of what he called *das Man,* a useful German expression that roughly means *they* (as in remarks such as "They say that you can't believe what you read in the newspapers"). Who are "they"? No one at all, says Heidegger—just an anonymous no one—used to lend credence to some supposed majority or group-mind to which it is safe to conform.

Noam Chomsky, in contemporary America, sees individualism as threatened by growing power centers within the system that he calls "state capitalism." To him the new situation is far from classical liberalism (à la the Enlightenment), and he sees the individual disappearing in this new system that he calls "highly authoritarian." It is hard for the person to live authentically, freely—or existentially—in the midst of these growing centers of public and state power and control. Individuals, he believes, are no more than "malleable cogs in this highly constrained machine."

Taking Chomsky's ideas into the sphere of journalism, we can see press centers of power (media conglomerates, groups, and chains) combining with government centers of power to restrain journalism from being truly oriented to the individual media units.

On the microscopic level where the journalists work within the media institutions, individual journalists have little freedom as they find themselves controlled and directed constantly by press system authorities. And, at this level, the journalists are not protected by the First Amendment—being only functionaries or hirelings of some entrepreneurial enterprise.

But this depersonalization or group-affinity cannot be blamed on the "power centers"; the journalists *themselves acquiesce in it.* In fact, as Erich Fromm and others have pointed out, people desire to escape from freedom because of the trauma attached to making decisions. This sense of safety in groups where the "system" decides is what existentialists warn against. Persons who attempt to escape freedom are living inauthentic lives, are not "creating selves," and are in fact living "in bad faith." In spite of the enticements of parentalism or social control, freedom (especially positive freedom—*not being passive*) is needed in a society that is open, where diversity and pluralistic journalism are important.

The existential journalist will fight against passivity, against encroaching corporate control, against conformity and robotization, against group-mindedness, and against debilitating inertia that saps the human spirit. For the existential journalist, freedom means freedom for all; journalistic authenticity should exist for all. Journalistic responsibility is individually determined, but it is determined always with others in mind. Although the uniqueness of each person is valued, the existential journalist cares about the society in which these unique persons reside. The existential journalist is no isolated hermit unattached to the world. In fact, of all people, the existentialist is an *involver,* a participator, an actor—constantly committing and risking so that a more vital and meaningful life will be developed.

The Importance of Subjectivity

Largely subjective, existential journalism places great stress on the *person* who creates journalism. But the world "out there" in all its complexity, its dangers and opportunities, is not ignored. This objective world of reality is taken seriously by the existential journalist; it is simply that the *perception* of this objective world is stressed, with much emphasis placed on the journalist as the creator of the verbal and symbolic world used to reflect the real one. Such existential subjectivism is not extreme; rather, it is temperate, endowing journalism with a personal perspective while retaining a reasonableness and a moderation needed for a credible demeanor.

This reasonableness does, indeed, impinge on both freedom and subjectivity, limiting both to some degree; but this in itself contributes to existential journalism's being a moderate stance. Yes, the spirit, the emotions, and the subjective elements of the journalist are stressed, but this does not mean that reason has been thrown out. The mind guides and tempers the emotions and the restless, adventurous nature. Although the passions and the subjective spirit of the existential journalist may be the guiding force, reason harnesses this force and keeps it under control.

The concept of objectivity is, of course, important in journalism, and the existentialist pays it proper due. But subjectivity must not be suppressed. The journalist is a subjective creature, largely filtering reality through perceptive screens. She assumes a false nature when trying too hard to become a detached and completely neutral reflector of events. Erich Fromm has insisted that objectivity is not the same as detachment or aloofness; it means having *an interest in* what is being dealt with, involving one's self fully in the observation of the event and bringing to bear on it the totality of one's values, insights, and perceptions.

Truth in the objective sense will never emerge in journalism. The existential journalist knows that his or her perceptions and evaluations are what will emerge. This does not mean that he or she is unconcerned about the reality of the event, thing, or person; it simply means that straining this reality "out there" through the subjective reportorial process is not to be considered harmful or dangerous—nor it is necessarily counterproductive to the emergence of the truth. The existential journalist knows this: There is no way to separate self from story, and as the story becomes ever more controversial and complex, this basic journalistic principle becomes ever more obvious.

Making Use of Freedom

Journalists of the existentialist type are users of freedom. And they are expanders of freedom. Not content to sit on their freedom, they constantly attempt to push back the limits of control, to take advantage of the degree of freedom they have, and to defend their freedom against the many forces that attempt to restrict it. The operative word for the existential journalist is *use* of freedom—or doing something with the opportunities that freedom permits. And *expanding* freedom is also important, and in such expansion the existentialist in journalism exemplifies an other-directed, altruistic concern. So it should be clear that existentialists are not self-indulging, strictly autonomous journalists who do not think of others.

Such journalists use their freedom constantly; they are vital, dynamic, passionate, and committed. They are sickened by conformist, stagnant, routine, passive, and uncommitted journalism. Thrusting themselves into the social maelstrom, they seek to harmonize their own self-interest with the wider public interest. But *they* want to do it, not doing it as part of some group-directed enterprise. The reclusive journalist who lives in a private world is not an existential journalist. Existentialism demands that a journalist push forward, experiment, explore, take chances, and try to make a difference in the world. Freedom allows this. This is why freedom is so important to the existential journalist.

As has been stressed in earlier chapters of this book, the existential journalist rebels against being a cog in the wheel of journalism, preferring to emphasize a uniqueness of character—and desiring to project this character into society through journalism. Rebelling against being anonymous and lost in journalism, the existentialist prizes freedom used responsibly and takes great pride in personal decision-making. In short, the existential journalist values and desires self-respect and authenticity—the attendants of freedom.

The Three A's of Existentialism

In closing this final chapter, consider what might be called the "three A's" of existential journalism. They are *anxiety, alienation,* and *authenticity*—three of existentialism's most pervasive themes. The first two are negative and harmful, or pose psychological hurdles for the journalist. The third (authenticity) is positive and helps the existentialist conquer the first two.

Tied closely to anxiety are such feelings as dread, concern, fear, and pessimism. And related to alienation are feelings of isolation, loss of self, personal insignificance, and impotence in the face of corporate power and size. The existential journalist has to battle constantly against anxiety and alienation in order to retain dignity, sanity, and a balanced life. In this battle, the existential journalist must call upon, and develop, authenticity. This authenticity demands that journalists respect themselves, act honestly and forthrightly, and choose self-satisfying action. Only when this is accomplished can anxiety and alienation be held at bay.

First, let us look at *anxiety*. The journalist is anxious, buffeted by a sense of dread, of anguish—*Angst,* as the Germans call it. This anxiety comes from the traumatic nature of freedom, a freedom that forces the conscientious journalist to choose and accept personal responsibility for the outcome of these choices. It is an anxiety born of uncertainty, of the recognition of personal inadequacies and limitations—and ultimately, of the shortness of life. The existential journalist, being a person of strong sensitivities and emotions and being conscientious, is prone to anxiety.

Second, there is *alienation* that causes problems for the existential journalist. At least it is "a sense" of alienation—the fact that the journalist senses an isolation from society in the reporter's role. Such journalists often feel they are no more than pawns in the hands of some power structure, restricted to routinized activities. It is thereby difficult for such journalists to retain their own selfhood or identity as they routinely gather, package, and transmit the real world to others.

The third major A is *authenticity,* which is the escape hatch from the negativism of the first two A's. Being authentic can lead the journalist to harmony, hope, optimism, and progress; it is the positive A. Authenticity is probably the supreme virtue of existentialism. Too often journalists in the newsroom are subsumed in the corporate machine, their freedom and individualism highly regulated and limited. They find themselves putting on false selves in order to cope, to adapt, to progress; they too often find that inauthenticity pays off and authenticity causes them social pain. So they push their real selves over into the shadows, and they do it so often that finally they do not know who they are. The existentialist, on the other hand, prizes authenticity and is conscious of his or her real self.

Carpe Diem, Journalist!

So the existential journalist will determine to get out of the shadows, live authentically, shake off the angst, and rebel against alienation that comes with losing one's self in the corporate entity. I feel certain that there are many who will *never* think existential journalism is important. They will, in all probability, continue ignoring such "useless" concepts and thinking they may even be somewhat antisocial, counterproductive, and even dangerous. Or, they may redefine existential journalism in their own words so that the fundamental ingredients as discussed on these pages will be lost in a more "cooperative and socially relevant" context.

On the other hand, I know that the orientation described here—one which I am calling "existential journalism," will appeal to many persons. Quite likely, they will be the already converted—the existentialists who recognize the validity, the authenticity, the self-satisfaction, and daily challenge that come with such an orientation applied to journalistic activities.

This book is substantially the same as the first edition, published in 1977. In the two decades since its publication, numerous persons—many of them former students now working as journalists—have attested to the benefits and inspiration offered in these pages. This volume is designed for such students, and for jaded and dissatisfied practicing journalists who may stumble across it. I hope that these pages will open new and interesting vistas of thought for existentialists and nonexistentialists alike, and that dialogue in an area that I think is the most important in journalism today will be expanded.

It is time to exit the stultifying cocoon of conformity, to break ranks and take the existential plunge into the swirling waters of new experiences. It is time to recognize the importance of *carpe diem*; it is time to seize the moment with vigor, faith, dedication, and a firm sense of responsibility.

BIBLIOGRAPHY

Allen, E. L. *From Plato to Nietzsche*. Greenwich, Conn.: Fawcett Publications—a Premier Book, 1964.

Anderson, Jack. *The Anderson Papers*. New York: Random House—Ballentine Books, 1974.

Aranguren, J. L. *Human Communication*. Trans. by Frances Partridge. New York: McGraw-Hill, 1967.

Bagdikian, Ben. *The Effete Conspiracy and Other Crimes by the Press*. New York: Harper & Row—Colophon Books, 1974.

Barnes, Hazel. *An Existentialist Ethics*. New York: Random House—Vintage Books, 1971.

Barrett, William. *Irrational Man: A Study in Existential Philosophy*. New York: Doubleday Anchor Books, 1962.

––––––. *What is Existentialism?* New York: Grove Press, 1964.

Beauvoir, Simone de. *The Ethics of Ambiguity*. Trans. by Bernard Frechtman. Secaucus, N.J.: The Citadel Press, 1972.

Bell, A. Donald, and J. C. Merrill. *Dimensions of Christian Writing*. Grand Rapids, Mich.: Zondervan Publishing House, 1970.

Berger, Peter L. *Invitation to Sociology: A Humanistic* Perspective. Garden City, N.Y.: Doubdleday Anchor Books, 1963.

Bode, Carl (ed.). *The Portable Thoreau*. New York: The Viking Press, 1947.

Brajnovic, Luka. *Deontología Periodística*. Pamplona: Ediciones Universidad de Navarra, S.A., 1969.

Brée, Germaine. *Camus and Sartre: Crisis and Commitment*. New York: Dell Publishing Co.—a Delta Book, 1972.

Buber, Martin. *Between Man and Man*. Trans. by R. G. Smith. New York: The Macmillan Co., 1972.

Burnier, Michel-Antoine. *Choice of Action: The French Existentialists on the Political Front Line*. Trans. by B. Murchland. New York: Vintage Books, 1969.

Bury, J. B. *The Idea of Progress*. New York: The Macmillan Co., 1932.

Camus, Albert. *The Myth of Sisyphus & Other Essays*. Trans. by Justin O'Brien. New York: Vintage Books, 1955.

———. *The Rebel*. New York: Alfred Knopf, Inc., and Random House—Vintage Books, 1954.

———. *Resistance, Rebellion, and Death*. Trans. by Justin O'Brien. New York: Random House—Vintage Books, 1961.

———. *The Stranger*. New York: Vintage Books, 1946.

Collins, James. *The Mind of Kierkegaard*. Chicago: Henry Regnery Co.—a Gateway Edition, 1967.

Danto, Arthur C. *Jean-Paul Sartre*. New York: The Viking Press, 1975.

Dennis, Everette E. and William L. Rivers. *Other Voices: The New Journalism in America*. San Francisco: The Canfield Press, 1974.

Ellul, Jacques. *Propaganda*. New York: Vintage Books, 1973.

Epstein, Edward J. *Between Fact and Fiction: The Problem of Journalism*. New York: Random House—Vintage Books, 1975.

Frankel, Charles. *The Case for Modern Man*. Boston: Beacon Press, 1971.

Frings, Manfred S. (ed.). *Heidegger and the Quest for Truth*. Chicago: Quadrangle Books, 1968.

Fromm, Erich. *Escape from Freedom*. New York: Avon Books, 1965.

———. *Man for Himself*. Greenwich, Conn.: A Fawcett Premier Book, 1966.

———. *The Revolution of Hope*. New York: Harper & Row, 1968.

Gardner, John W. *Excellence*. New York: Harper & Row—Perennial Library, 1971.

Grene, Marjorie. *Introduction to Existentialism*. Chicago: University of Chicago Press, 1970.

Harris, Sydney J. *The Authentic Person: Dealing with Dilemma*. Niles, Ill.: Argus Communications, 1972.

Heinemann, F. H. *Existentialism and the Modern Predicament*. New York: Harper Torchbooks, 1958.

Hill, Brian V. *Education and the Endangered Individual*. New York: Dell Publishing Co., 1973.

Hoffer, Eric. *The True Believer*. New York: Mentor Books, 1962.

Horvath, Nicholas A. *Philosophy*. Woodbury, N.Y.: Barron's Educational Series, Inc., 1974.

Huizinga, Johan. *Homo Ludens*. Boston: Beacon Press, 1955.

Husserl, Edmund. *Cartesian Meditations*. The Hague: Nijhoff, 1960.

Huxley, Aldous. *Brave New World Revisited*. New York: Harper & Row—Perennial Library, 1965.

Jaspers, Karl. *Man in the Modern Age*. Garden City, N.Y.: Doubleday Anchor Books, 1957.

———. *Neitzsche: An Introduction to the Understanding of His Philosophical Activity*. Chicago: Henry Regnery Co.—a Gateway Edition, 1969.

Johnson, Michael L. *The New Journalism*. Lawrence: University of Kansas Press, 1971.

Jung, Carl G. *The Undiscovered Self.* New York: Mentor Books, 1958.

Jung, Hwa Yol (ed.). *Existential Phenomenology and Political Theory: A Reader.* Chicago: Henry Regnery Co., 1972.

Kaplan, Abraham. *The New World of Philosophy.* New York: Vintage Books, 1961.

Kaufmann, Walter (ed.). *Existentialism from Dostoevsky to Sartre.* New York: New American Library—Medidian Books, 1975.

Kierkegaard, Søren. *Fear and Trembling* and *The Sickness unto Death.* Trans. by Walter Lowrie. Princeton: Princeton University Press, 1968.

―――. *The Present Age.* New York: Harper Torchbooks, 1962.

Klein, J. F. *The Physical Significance of Entropy.* New York: D. Van Nostrand Co., 1919.

Koestenbaum, Peter. *Philosophy: A General Introduction.* New York: American Book Co., 1968.

Kuhns, William. *The Post-Industrial Prophets: Interpretations of Technology.* New York: Harper Colophon Books, 1971.

Macquarrie, John. *Existentialism.* Baltimore: Penguin Books, 1973.

Mannheim, Karl. *Ideology and Utopia.* New York: Harcourt Brace and Co., 1936.

Mansur, Anthony. *Sartre: a Philosophic Study.* New York: Oxford University Press, 1967.

Marcel, Gabriel. *Man Against Mass Society.* Chicago: Henry Regnery Co.—a Gateway Edition, 1969.

―――. *The Philosophy of Existentialism.* Trans. by Manya Harari. New York: The Citadel Press, 1968.

Marcuse, Herbert. *One-Dimensional Man.* Boston: Beacon Press, 1966.

McLuhan, Marshall. *Understanding Media: The Extensions of Man.* New York: McGraw-Hill Paperbacks, 1965.

McQuail, Denis (ed.). *Sociology of Mass Communications.* Baltimore: Penguin Books, 1972.

Mencken, H. L. *A Gang of Pecksniffs.* Edited by Theo Lippman, Jr. New Rochelle, N.Y.: Arlington House, 1975.

Merleau-Ponty, Maurice. *Adventures of the Dialectic.* Trans. by Joseph Bien. Evanston: Northwestern University Press, 1973.

―――. *Phenomenology of Perception.* Trans. by Colin Smith. London: Routledge & Kegan Paul, 1962.

Merrill, John C. *The Imperative of Freedom: A Philosophy of Journalistic Autonomy.* New York: Hastings House, 1974.

Merrill, John C., and Ralph L. Lowenstein. *Media, Messages, and Men.* New York: David McKay, 1971.

Meyer, Philip. *Precision Journalism: A Reporter's Introduction to Social Scientific Methods.* Bloomington: Indiana University Press, 1973.

Middleton, Neil (ed.). *The I. F. Stone's Weekly Reader.* New York: Vintage Books, 1974.

Mills, C. Wright. *Power, Politics and People*. New York: Ballantine Books, 1962.

Morgan, George W. *The Human Predicament*. New York: Dell Publishing Co.—a Delta Books, 1970.

Mumford, Lewis. *Transformations of Man*. New York: Harper Torchbooks, 1972.

Needham, Joseph. *Time: The Refreshing River*. New York: Macmillan, 1943.

Nietzsche, Friedrich. *The Birth of Tragedy* and *The Case of Wagner*. Trans. by Walter Kaufmann. New York: Vintage Books, 1967.

_____. *On the Genealogy of Morals* and *Ecce Homo*. Trans. by Walter Kaufmann. New York: Vintage Books, 1967.

_____. *Twilight of the Idols* and *The Anti-Christ*. Trans. by R. J. Hollingdale. Baltimore: Penguin Books, 1974.

Novack, George (ed.). *Existentialism versus Marxism*. New York: Dell Publishing Co.—Delta Books, 1966.

Novak, Michael. *Belief and Unbelief: A Philosophy of Self-Knowledge*. New York: Mentor-Omega Books, 1965.

_____. *The Experience of Nothingness*. New York: Harper Colophon Books, 1971.

Olson, Robert G. *An Introduction to Existentialism*. New York: Dover Publications, Inc., 1962.

Ortega y Gasset, José. *Man and People*. New York: W. W. Norton & Co., 1963.

_____. *Mission of the University*. New York: W. W. Norton & Co.—The Norton Library, 1944.

Patka, Frederick (ed.). *Existentialist Thinkers and Thought*. New York: The Citadel Press, 1966.

Poole, Roger, *Towards Deep Subjectivity*. New York: Harper Trochbooks, 1972.

Riesman, David. *The Lonely Crowd*. New Haven: Yale University Press, 1961.

Roubiczek, Paul. *Existentialism: For and Against*. Cambridge: Cambridge University Press, 1966.

Russell, Bertrand. *Authority and the Individual*. Boston: Beacon Press, 1960.

_____. *The Will to Doubt*. New York: Philosophical Library—the Wisdom Library, 1958.

Sartre, Jean-Paul. *Being and Nothingness*. New York: Philosophical Library, 1956.

_____. *Existentialism and Human Emotions*. New York: Philosophical Library, 1957.

_____. *Situations*. Trans. by Nenita Eisler. Greenwich, Conn.: A Fawcett Premier Book, 1965.

Schiller, Herbert I. *Mass Communications and American Empire*. Boston: Beacon Press, 1971.

Seidenberg, Roderick. *Posthistoric Man: An Inquiry.* New York: Viking Press, 1974.

Solomon, Robert C. (ed.). *Phenomenology and Existentialism.* New York: Harper & Row, 1972.

Solzhenitsyn, Alexander. *From Under the Rubble.* New York: Bantam Books, 1975.

Sorokin, Pitirim A. *Modern Historical and Social Philosophies.* New York: Dover Publications, Inc., 1963.

Spengler, Oswald. *The Decline of the West.* New York: Alfred A. Knopf, Inc., 1926.

————. *Selected Essays.* Trans. by Donald O. White. Chicago: Henry Regnery Co.—a Gateway Edition, 1967.

Streller, Justus. *To Freedom Condemned: A Guide to the Philosophy of Jean-Paul Sartre.* New York: Philosophical Library—the Wisdom Library, 1960.

Tebbel, John. *The Media in America.* New York: New American Library—Mentor Books, 1976.

Trilling, Lionel. *Sincerity and Authenticity.* Cambridge: Harvard University Paperback, 1972.

Tuccille, Jerome. *Radical Libertarianism.* New York: Perennial Library, 1971.

Van Over, Raymond (ed.). *The Psychology of Freedom.* Greenwich, Conn.: Fawcett Premier Books, 1974.

Volkman, A. D. (ed.). *Thoreau on Man and Nature.* Mt. Vernon, N.Y.: The Peter Pauper Press, 1960.

Wahl, Jean. *A Short History of Existentialism.* New York: Philosophical Library, 1949.

White, Morton. *Social Thought in America: The Revolt Against Formalism.* Boston: Beacon Press, 1957.

Wiener, Norbert. *The Human Use of Human Beings: Cybernetics and Society.* New York: Avon Books—Discus Edition, 1967.

Wolfe, Tom. *The New Journalism.* New York: Harper & Row, 1973.

Wylie, Philip. *The Magic Animal.* New York: Simon & Schuster—Pocket Books, 1969.

Yablonsky, Lewis. *Robopaths: People as Machines.* Baltimore: Penguin Books, 1972.

INDEX